Munich

first lady of america
a romanticized biography of
POCAHONTAS

first lady of america
a romanticized biography of
POCAHONTAS
by Leon Phillips
foreword by Clifford Dowdey

Westover
Publishing Company

Richmond, Virginia
A Media General Publication

Books by Leon Phillips

The First Lady of America, a Romanticized Biography of Pocahontas

The Fantastic Breed: Americans in King George's War

Split Bamboo

Queen's Blade

When the Wind Blows

SBN 0-87858-033-6

For
Anne Brennan

Foreword

Pocahontas is one of those historical characters who comes across to us eternally embalmed in some legend, rather than as a person in her own right and in her own humanity. The legend of the Indian maiden saving the life of a British adventurer to the New World is, of course, most beguiling, the very essence of romance. Whether or not the legend is true—in whole or in part or not at all—it has obscured the real story of a very remarkable young woman who happened to be the first Indian princess of the New World known to the English-speaking people and to their history.

Significantly for her real story, this fascinating young woman was known to the Virginia Colony and to London without a hint of any legend, but entirely for herself. In this book, Mr. Phillips presents us with what might be called the historical Pocahontas: freed from her legendary appendage to Captain John Smith's brief stay in the Colony, Pocahontas is revealed in her own complete life story.

Mr. Phillips shows a historical Pocahontas full of contradictions. In many aspects of her personality, she comes across to us as the equivalent of a modern woman, strong willed and independent minded; yet, in her background she was the product of an ancient, traditional culture, of a proud and powerful people. However, being a princess, and the apple of the eye of old Powhatan, the great chief of chiefs, Pocahontas was not typical of the Indian culture which formed her.

In our time, some imagination is required to free our conception of American Indians from the impressions formed by countless motion-pictures and television offerings depicting the plains Indians. These continuously mounted warriors toiled not and devoted their time exclusively to futile chases of stagecoaches or to commiting suicide by riding in circles around wagon trains. They existed totally in relation to whites. By contrast, the Atlantic Coast Indians of the confederation ruled by Powhatan had never seen a white until Pocahontas was twelve years old, and the tribes—whose demesne stretched from north of Virginia to south of Virginia, from the coast to the mountains—felt no immediate threat from the small band clinging perilously for survival on Jamestown Island.

Regarding the strangers with a mixture of curiosity and hostility, Powhatan's people continued the cultivation of their fields and villages. An agrarian people rather than hunters like the plains Indians (although they also hunted), the Chickahominy nation were successful farmers. They "stored grains, dried and salted meats and dried vegetables in bins or silos built on high ground behind the main town..." on the site of the present city of Richmond. The smaller communities followed the same practices. They lived in huts and built large chambers in which the governing council met. While the nation was so powerful that all of its scattered tribes were safe from enemies, the bucks continued to train for war as they had during the days when their warriors established dominance in their region. They were a fine looking people, copper-skinned and standing very straight, and inordinately vain of their appearance. Male and female, old and young, all dressed skimpily.

Following Pocahontas from her earliest days, Mr. Phillips shows how she used the privileges of being the youngest daughter of the mighty Chief to defy many of the customs of the tradition-bound society. She liked to dress as a boy, occasionally accompanied one of her brothers on hunting excursions, and developed the prowess of a brave in throwing an ax and shooting an arrow. Her behavior was so tomboyish and uninhibited that she shocked the tough English colonists when, at sixteen, she first visited Jamestown with her father.

Even more than the average woman of her race, she held the warriors in contempt because of their idleness. Mr. Phillips advances the plausible theory that she admired the contrasting energy and ambition of the British settlers. Later in London, after she had been uprooted from her own tranquil world, Pocahontas had become "resilient and independent to a degree unknown in the civilization of the Old World."

She was to need these qualities, plus courage and a bubbling sense of humor which, although not usually associated in our minds with Indians, was commonplace among Powhatan's people.

From the Jamestown settlement in 1607 until 1611, when Pocahontas was sixteen, relations worsened between the colonists and the Indians. As the Colony grew and expeditions became more frequent outside its triangular fortified area, Powhatan and his chiefs began to feel threatened by the encroachment into their homeland. Though the councils were divided over specific policy, some of the chiefs advocating immediate war, the general attitude of the chiefs, including especially Powhatan, had turned into forthright hostility. As the English in turn grew apprehensive over Powhatan's aggressive intentions, one of their leaders, hard-bitten Captain Samuel Argall, arrived at a pragmatic expedient. Through trickery and surprise, he captured Pocahontas, bringing her to Jamestown, where as a hostage she was held as a guarantee of peace from her anxious father.

Mr. Phillips reveals Pocahontas' remarkable adaptiveness by developing the details of her stay in Jamestown. She was taken into the home of Sir Thomas Dale, the deputy Governor, and Lady Dale, where she was accepted as a ward. Never made to feel either an oddity or a captive, the naturally attractive girl was treated as if she were a young kinswoman on an extended visit. If the adaptation was difficult, and if at times she longed for her native life, the evidence shows that slowly and apparently painlessly Pocahontas became to a considerable degree anglicized.

The language barrier was overcome by either one or both of the rectors, Mister Hunt and Mister Buck, who successively represented the Established Church in Jamestown. While the churchmen instructed Pocahontas for a conversion to Christianity, they taught her English in the then new King James' translation of the Bible, and thus she spoke the most beautiful English ever written. Two years after she came to Jamestown, Pocahontas was baptized into the Anglican Communion.

A Christian, anglicized and eighteen years old, Pocahontas was then ready for an English marriage. Had she married an Indian, her husband would have had to be the son of a chief. Since no titled Englishmen had settled permanently in Jamestown, the most acceptable suitor to her guardian-advisers was a man of substance, John Rolfe. Educated (an Oxford graduate) and of substantial background, he was not among those adventurers who had come to Virginia for quick riches, but on sizeable holdings Rolfe had planted the first commercially profitable tobacco and opened the way for future fortunes on the "golden leaf." A widower with two young children, Rolfe was a grave, dignified gentleman of approximately thirty, which in those days made him seem almost middle-aged, but he conceived a most passionate attachment to Pocahontas. He found favor with Pocahontas and she married him in 1614, when nineteen.

They lived in a house he built for them in Jamestown and, bearing a son after one year, Pocahontas was a good conventional wife, even if all her ways (such as swimming in the river) were not conventional by English standards. With her new learning, she undertook the education of her own child and her two step-children, and for two years the family seemed as comfortably happy as the next.

In Pocahontas' twenty-first year, the Rolfe's journeyed to London, and Mr. Phillips projects the ultimate drama in Pocahontas' life as it unfolded in the fashionable world of London. Only five years removed from her relatively primitive wilderness life, when she was presented first to formal society and then to the court, the handsome copper-skinned girl won the hearts of all with her charm and manners, her speech and dress, and perhaps most of all, her luminous personality. Though obviously something of an oddity, Pocahontas won the respect and admiration of British nobility in her own person and the simple people of London nearly mobbed her when she went on the streets. As the daughter of a chief,

Pocahontas took the adulation for granted and remained unaffected by it all.

However, as time passed and she suffered the adverse affects of the climate, Pocahontas began to long for Virginia. Here her story turned tragic, for she never again saw her native land.

In making this book the personal story of Pocahontas, Mr. Phillips has presented her against vividly drawn backgrounds of her three worlds—the Indian wilderness, the Jamestown colonizing settlement and the post-Elizabethan society of London. In this splendid panorama, the Indian princess personalizes and dramatizes the meeting of the Old World and the New World in England's first successful attempt at settlement.

C. D.

I

Now there were no more foes, and each year, when the
first buds appeared on the limbs of the great tree, the
Chickahominy carved another notch in the bark and then
celebrated the era of peace wrought by the wise Powhatan.
The traditions of the people were strong, but Powhatan had
been even stronger, and in breaking them had forged a new
age. Demonstrating his unique code of living for the first time
at the conclusion of his war with the Tutelo, he had killed no
prisoners, taken none of the enemy's women into his own
tribe, enslaved neither warriors nor their sons and exacted no
tribute of corn, walnuts, coarse barley, groundnuts or wild

cherries. Instead he had offered the losers friendship, asking in return only that they pledge fealty to him and join him in his campaign to impose a lasting peace on other belligerent tribes. Other tribes, as will be seen, fared less well at his hands.

The strategy had been repeated many times, and for five springs before Pocahontas's birth the entire area had been at peace. That was why delegations from many nations brought gifts of treated deerskin, carved bone ornaments and toys, jerked venison and smoked fish to the daughter of Powhatan. From the north came the representatives of the Lenape and the Nanticoke, from the northwest the senior warriors of the once-ferocious Conoy, from the south the councillors of the Pimlico and the Tutelo.

Rawhide drums carried the news to distant nations that were not associated with the Confederation, and they, too, sent their congratulations to the Chickahominy Chief of Chiefs. From the land of the great Cherokee Confederation, on the far side of the mountains that looked blue in the haze of early evening, came two sons of the Sachem of that great people. From the deep south came the principal warrior of the fierce Tuscarora, a nation that would be driven far to the north by the invaders from across the sea and would join the league of the Iroquois in order to protect themselves. The appearance of a representative of the Tuscarora, the traditional enemy of the Chickahominy, was something of a surprise, and Powhatan agreed with the members of his Council that, inasmuch as the principal warrior himself had made the journey, he might be curious about the strength of the Chickahominy.

So, for his benefit, the hosts staged mock war games that were usually held only to celebrate the birth of a chief's son. Five hundred young braves demonstrated their prowess shooting at targets with their bows and arrows, hurling hatchets and knives made of metal obtained deep in the interior at saplings until the trees were felled. The exhibition was impressive, particularly because it was carried out in disciplined unison by warriors from all six of the tribes that made up the Chickahominy Confederation.

The principal warrior of the Tuscarora observed all that he was shown, complimented his hosts and departed.

Powhatan took no unnecessary chances, and for the first time in several years lookout posts were reestablished in the treetops on the borders of the Confederation's territory, but no attack developed. The Tuscarora displayed the wisdom born of discretion, and all the people of the Chickahominy and their allies hailed the daughter of Powhatan as the bearer of good fortune and the maiden of peace. So Pocahontas enjoyed a favored position from the very beginning of her life, unusual for a girl child, even the daughter of the Chief of Chiefs.

In the year 1595, as men on the far shores of the Great Sea recorded the passage of time, a girl child was born in the principal town of the Chickahominy on the banks of what would become known as the James River in Virginia, about fifty miles inland from its mouth. Ordinarily the birth of a girl would have created little interest and less excitement, but this child was the only daughter of Powhatan, the great statesman and warrior, lifelong leader of his people, who had formed the Chickahominy Confederation, a league of many tribes that had dominion as far north as the land that would become Pennsylvania and deep into the country to the south that the invaders would call North Carolina.

As was the custom, the girl was given two names: within the confines of her family she would be known as Matoaka, but to outsiders she would be Pocahontas. Thanks in part to a legend that had no basis in fact she would be remembered in story and poetry for hundreds of years, but her real claim to immortality was more elusive, more subtle. Although it is unlikely that she or any of her contemporaries realized it, she was a symbol of eternal womanhood, one who could make her way, prosper and find contentment in three different civilizations, each of them totally dissimilar to the other two.

Her father may have been the most prominent American Indian of his era on the Atlantic seaboard, a man whose efforts had won him lasting renown in his own world long before English settlers disrupted his society. He achieved so much, in fact, that after his death his tribe took his name and thereafter were called the Powhatan. The mother of Pocahontas is unknown, but from what Pocahontas told her good friend, Lady de la Warr, wife of Jamestown's governor, many years later, her mother was the second of Powhatan's three wives. The first, the mother of the two sons of the Chief of Chiefs, Mataoko and Piaoko, having died several years earlier, Powhatan took a second wife, and it was she who died in childbirth when Pocahontas came into the world of the silent forests.

These deep woods of yellow pine and hickory, walnut and poplar, hemlock and cedar and chestnut were not really silent. That was a myth fostered by the newcomers from the far lands across the sea, but Mataoko and Piaoko knew better, and Pocahontas would learn they were right. When one knew how to listen, one could distinguish the faint sounds made by animals, and could even distinguish the rustle of the fox from that of the porcupine or raccoon. Great, lumbering bears, indifferent to the proximity of lesser breeds, crashed through the forest underbrush, and so did the wild boar. Only the deer, the rabbit and the wildcat were truly silent.

The town of the Chickahominy had expanded enormously during the nineteen springs of Powhatan's leadership, and at the time of his daughter's birth numbered approximately two thousand men, women and children. Like the people of other civilizations, the Chickahominy measured and recorded the passage of time in their own way. Nineteen springs earlier, when Powhatan had won his great victory in combat against the Tutelo, a tribe that had claimed kinship with the Tuscarora who lived still farther to the south, a notch had been cut in the massive trunk of the towering oak in the center of the then tiny Chickahominy village, a tree whose main branches had been used by the tribe's senior warriors as lookout stations when they had maintained their eternal, vigilant watch for their enemies.

It was not accidental that the Chickahominy dominated the Confederation. Nature had seen to that, and most likely they would have assumed leadership in the area even if the hard-driving Powhatan had never lived. Most of the North American aborigines, like the men of Europe, were surprisingly short, and even the braves of the most warlike of the northern nations, the Seneca, were no taller than five feet six or seven inches, approximately the same height as the settlers who would come to the New World in such large numbers during the seventeenth century. The Chickahominy were among the tallest and huskiest of Indians, and stood two to three inches higher than most of their contemporaries.

They had lived on the James River for as long as their sages could remember, and their villages on the shores of what would become Chesapeake Bay had been there for generations, they and the gentle, fish-consuming Chesapeake nation having reached an agreement to respect each others territorial rights. Perhaps the greatest strength of the Chickahominy, like that of the Cherokee beyond the mountains, lay in the fact that they were an agrarian people who enjoyed the benefits of a stable economy. Most Indian tribes subsisted on game, supplemented by wild fruits and roots, and when the vagaries of the weather drove animals out of an area, it became necessary to raid a neighboring tribe in order to gain possession of their food reserves.

Powhatan's people actually tilled the soil, however, and the farmlands lying outside the perimeter of their principal town may have occupied as much as several hundred acres. Their chief crop was corn, which they dried in the sun and stored in silos of clay they built on stiltlike contraptions above the surface of the ground. As many as three hundred women of the principal town worked in the cornfields. The Chickahominy also may have been among the first to cultivate the wild barley they found on high ground in the back country, and they stored quantities of it.

Root vegetables, among them carrots and onions, which grew in abundance near the banks of the James River, also formed an important part of the nation's diet. It is uncertain, however, whether these vegetables were cultivated or were gathered by searching parties of children; in all probability the latter was the case. It is believed that the Chickahominy and other nations of the area also ate potatoes, which had found their way from South America to the Northern Hemisphere in some mysterious way that neither scientists nor historians have as yet been able to deduce. Any potatoes the women and children dug up were unquestionably wild, however, and were much smaller than the potatoes grown by the English settlers a half-century later.

Walnuts and groundnuts, or peanuts, were also important to the Chickahominy, the latter having been introduced to them by the Tutelo. They were easy to grow, required little care and were stored in their shells until needed. Walnuts were considered a delicacy, as were chestnuts, and were boiled, then chopped and fashioned into little cakes sweetened with wild honey. These cakes were a favorite of the children, and Pocahontas undoubtedly ate her share of them as a small girl.

Meat and fish were plentiful, Chickahominy hunters supplying the former, while the latter were obtained from the nation's smaller villages on the shores of the great bay. Only when there was venison in abundance did the Chickahominy eat fresh, roasted meat. It was the custom, under ordinary circumstances, to smoke meats and store them in thinly shredded strips; prepared in this way they would not spoil, particularly when kept in wooden bins between layers of aromatic, dried grasses. Only those members of the Confederation who lived near the sea ate fresh fish, including shellfish. Most of the Chickahominy followed the practice observed by the nations of the interior, smoking their fish but taking care to preserve it only for short periods. Many of the Europeans who came to the New World during the seventeenth century learned this custom from the Indians, and those who failed to observe it frequently suffered from severe gastrointestinal ailments.

Fruits were so abundant that the Chickahominy felt no need to cultivate them, and in the spring, summer and early autumn the children of the town were sent into the forest to collect large quantities, which were eaten raw. Wild strawberries, much smaller and sweeter than those grown in Europe, were found everywhere, and blueberry patches near the river were protected from the birds by nets woven of young vines. Wild cherries grew in the area, too, and the Chickahominy followed the example of the Pimlico and put scarecrows near stands of cherry trees to keep birds at a distance.

Turkey, ducks and geese abounded in season, but even the best hunters found it difficult to wing them with bows and arrows, so intricate snares made of vines were used to catch them. All fowl were eaten roasted, but the human consumption of birds' eggs in any form was strictly forbidden, the Indians believing that the contents of eggs were unclean. Birds' feathers were preserved and were used to decorate the cloaks of tribal leaders, but only chiefs, their families and the sages were permitted to wear such cloaks. Many years later, in London, Pocahontas recalled that she had owned a feathered cape in her childhood and donned it on ceremonial occasions.

The Chickahominy were industrious, but enjoyed many feast days and other holidays, largely because the men of the nation had so much time on their hands. The women did all of the work in the fields, butchered and smoked the meats and were responsible for the storage and preservation of all foods. They also made the clothes, so the braves had little to occupy them other than hunting, and their borders were so secure they found it unnecessary to practice their marksmanship.

The younger men and children engaged in competitive sports on holidays, and girls as well as boys participated. There were contests in running, jumping and swimming, and the favorite game, which defies accurate description, was played with a ball made of the bladder or skin of an animal and stuffed with grass. Few Englishmen of the age could swim, and when Pocahontas lived in Jamestown, the settlement founded on the coast when she was about thirteen years of age, her hosts were astonished because she was as much at home in the water as she was on land.

Boys and girls alike went naked—in warm weather— until their seventh spring, at which time they were introduced to a single garment made of woven reeds that resembled a loose-fitting, knee-length dress. Boys wore it belted, but it was considered bad luck for a girl to wear a belt since this would constrict her middle and might make her unfit for motherhood. For cold weather this garment was made of rawhide, and with it the older boys and girls wore calf-high, rawhide boots. Undergarments were unknown and, when the Chickahominy learned of them from the invaders early in the seventeenth century, were regarded as unnecessary.

At puberty children adopted the attire of adults. Boys

wore loincloths of rawhide, and in chilly weather dressed in two shirts, the inner of woven reeds and the outer of rawhide. The clothing of girls remained essentially unchanged, but at puberty they were permitted to decorate their heretofore unornamented dresses with beads, shells and, in the case of Pocahontas, feathers.

A girl was forbidden to marry or engage in premarital sexual intercourse for three springs after she reached puberty. This was the most stringent of taboos restricting a young woman, and those who disobeyed were forced to become prostitutes who served the unmarried men. At the end of the three-year period, however, a young woman was allowed to sleep with any man, and her conduct in no way impaired her future status as a wife. When the male members of her family decided she was ready for marriage, the eldest of them sat in front of his house and smoked a pipe. Since the Chickahominy smoked on no other occasion, this was a signal that the head of the family was prepared to entertain bids for his daughter, who became the property of her husband.

Tobacco was scarce in the region that, within a half-century, would become the world's leading producer of the plant, and what little there was grew wild. The Indians failed to recognize the commercial value of the crop. Strangely, the tobacco that became the foundation for a great industry was imported from the Bahamas the better part of a decade after Jamestown was settled.

The Chickahominy lived in substantial dwellings made of logs, the open spaces cemented with a mixture of clay and chopped reeds, and all windows and doors were covered with animal skins that had been treated with the sap of the gum tree to make them water-repellant. The roofs of houses were similarly treated.

It is unlikely that the daughter of Powhatan lived in her father's house, the Chief of Chiefs being obliged to observe the mores of his people. Each family occupied a circular compound, in the center of which stood a stone-lined pit used for cooking by the women and girls. The largest house was reserved for the head of the family, and no one, including the members of his immediate family, was permitted to enter it without his express permission. His wife—the Chickahominy were primarily monogamous, with exceptions that will be noted subsequently—occupied the house directly opposite his. Both dwellings were furnished with beds made of pine boughs, which were covered with woven mats, and the girl children of a family, Pocahontas included, were required to make these mats. Spare clothing was stored on wall pegs. The husband's weapons were kept in that portion of his dwelling farthest from the door, while the wife's cooking utensils, consisting of gourds and clay pots, rested just inside the door of her house.

The elderly and infirm members of a family had houses of their own in the family circle, and it was the duty of all others, including the head of the household, to care for them. Those who were ill or aged were required to perform no duties of their own.

Boys and girls were housed together until their seventh spring, then were segregated and placed in separate dwellings within the compound. At puberty they left the circle, the boys going to a long house where they would be taught to become junior warriors, the girls being sent to a long house for maidens, where they began to assume some of the responsibilities and work load of the older women.

The half-brothers of Pocahontas were older, so it may be that she occupied a hut of her own, sleeping on the ground from earliest childhood. Since her mother had died, it is probable that one or another of Powhatan's sisters took care of her; the precise number of his sisters is unknown, but all who were related to him were entitled to live in his compound, which was the largest in the community.

According to the standards of the Chickahominy, the daughter of Powhatan enjoyed privileges and luxuries denied girls whose fathers were ordinary braves. The English invaders whose coming would destroy the tranquility of the wilderness town would regard the childhood life of Pocahontas as primitive, but that was a relative judgment. What really mattered was that the girl became resilient and independent to a degree unknown in the civilization of the Old World. That was fortunate, because her future would require both courage and stamina.

II

The extent to which Pocahontas participated in the communal life of the Chickahominy during the better part of two decades she spent with her own people can only be guessed, although she herself provided a number of clues in her later conversations with Lady de la Warr, her friend and protectress. Her life was complicated by her royal lineage, and her privileges were offset, in many ways, by the isolation she necessarily suffered.

A community sustained itself, so most Indian villages were small, but the Chickahominy being an agrarian people, as already noted, their principal town may have been one of the largest on the Eastern seaboard of the United States. And its social structure was far more complex than most of the strangers who crossed the Great Sea, and who regarded the natives they encountered as primitive barbarians, ever realized.

At the top of the pyramid stood Powhatan, but he was no absolute ruler, and had he been a tyrant he would have been deposed. Later claims to the effect that Indian tribes enjoyed a form of democratic rule were totally false, such myths coming into being soon after the United States attained her independence from Great Britain. In essence the Indian nation was an oligarchy ruled by a parliament of nobles, and it was "democratic" only to the extent that one's membership in this group did not necessarily depend upon heredity. The heads of a few powerful families more or less automatically passed membership to their sons, but a senior warrior who displayed courage in battle and wisdom in counsel almost invariably was admitted to the group.

The religious head of the nation, who presided at various festivals and ceremonies, and who was known as the Bi-tan, held a permanent seat in the Council, and well may have been the second most important of Chickahominy. Much earlier in the tribe's development his position and that of the chief had been combined, but the powers of the two posts had been separated, probably during the reign of Powhatan's grandfather, when the nation had been engaged in a long war with the Tuscarora and the head of state had been forced to devote all of his time and energy to that struggle.

Most Indian tribes were nature worshippers, but the Chickahominy prayed to their ancestors, the founder of each family having been raised over the generations to the status of a deity. The temporal and religious heads of the nation were believed to be descended from the same root, and consequently had an ancestor-god whom they worshipped in common. But the religious leader enjoyed a privilege that was unique to him and his sons: they alone were permitted to be polygamous. Most were content to marry only one woman, finding it difficult and impractical to live with more than one, but Pocahontas's uncle, who was the Bi-tan throughout her early life, had three wives, the youngest of them only a few years older than the daughter of Powhatan.

A form of primogeniture was enforced, and the eldest son of the chief became head of the nation when his father died or became too old and feeble to rule wisely. Similarly, the eldest son of the Bi-tan by any of his wives became the next religious leader of the tribe. All sons of both men became members of the Council when they became senior warriors, which means they were at least twenty-five years of age and had demonstrated their courage and sagacity in battle and their courage in the hunt. Theoretically, at least, the son of a chief or Bi-tan who failed to live up to the standard expected of all braves would remain a junior warrior all his life, which was also the fate of lesser men who did not distinguish themselves.

A chief or Bi-tan could be deposed and demoted by the Council but Pocahontas told King James I of England that she had never heard of this disgrace being visited upon any of her ancestors. When a man reached the top, he became so powerful that no member of the ruling group wanted to risk becoming his enemy by trying to unseat him.

Meetings of the Council were held in a long house that stood in the compound of the Chief of Chiefs, and as this building could hold approximately twenty to thirty persons in comfort, according to the estimates of some of the early Jamestown settlers, it is assumed that the ruling oligarchy was made up of about that number.

Women were regarded as inferiors by most Indian nations, including the Chickahominy, and no female was allowed to enter the long house of the Council. Pocahontas, who was her father's favorite and was something of a tomboy, was an exception. It amused Powhatan to permit her to attend Council meetings as an observer, but on these occasions certain proprieties were observed, and she wore male attire. The deliberations bored her, members of the Chickahominy government sharing the propensity of all lawmakers for making long speeches, and her mind wandered during the interminable debates. She enjoyed dressing like a boy, however, and on a number of occasions she accompanied the younger of her brothers, Piaoko, on hunting excursions, a pastime ordinarily denied members of her sex.

All of the functions of government, executive, legislative and judicial, were performed for the entire

Chickahominy nation by Powhatan and the members of his Council, but this task was not as arduous as it may appear. Tradition was one of the strongest forces in any Indian tribe, and those who flouted it were ostracized by their neighbors for the rest of their lives, a punishment that persuaded members of the nation to engage in little or no antisocial behavior.

The two greatest problems faced by the Chickahominy were maintaining peace and accumulating enough food to prevent hunger. By Powhatan's time satisfactory solutions had been found to both. The nation was so strong that no other tribe or confederation of tribes dared to make war on them, and as farmers they were eminently successful, storing grains, dried and salted meats and dried vegetables in bins or silos built on high ground behind the main town. The smaller Chickahominy communities followed the same practice. And when the time came to decide whether to make war against the Jamestown settlers, Powhatan did not determine the question alone, but submitted to a consensus of his Council.

In day-to-day living the Chickahominy were easygoing, thus simplifying the task of the Council, which settled all major disputes between groups and individuals. Each family owned its own dwelling compound, and land was so plentiful there were no quarrels over real estate. When a young warrior married and wanted to establish his own home, he and his friends chopped down a few trees at the edge of the town, uprooted the stumps and built a hut there. Theft was a problem, men and women alike taking a casual view of private property. It was considered improper to steal within the nation, and as most families owned clothing, cooking utensils, weapons and toilet articles more or less identical to those of their neighbors, thefts occurred infrequently. When it was proved—usually by the common consent of one's neighbors—that a man or woman had stolen, the family was subjected to ostracization that was tantamount to isolation.

Murder within the ranks of the nation was virtually unknown as it was believed that one's ancestors frowned on such acts of violence committed against kinsmen. On the rare occasions when one Chickahominy killed another, the culprit was taken before the Bi-tan. A trial—in the sense of the men from across the sea—was unknown; the Bi-tan merely pronounced a predetermined, dreaded sentence: the killer was banished from the nation and was sent into the deep forests alone, without weapons. Presumably he eventually died of starvation.

Adultery was not regarded as either a crime or an antisocial act of lesser consequence. When a brave coveted his neighbor's wife, he took her, and when the duped husband learned the truth of the infidelity, he returned the compliment by having an affair with the lover's wife. No one seemed to mind and family life was uninterrupted, marital jealousy being beyond the ken of the Chickahominy. No stigma was attached to a single woman of sixteen who took one or more lovers, although, as previously noted, those who engaged in acts of intercourse at an earlier age were forced to become prostitutes for the rest of their lives. Only a bachelor could commit the cardinal sexual sin: the single man who had an affair with a married woman was subjected to severe punishment, precisely the same as that meted out to warriors who displayed cowardice in battle. The details will be discussed in a later chapter. It must be assumed that the punishment was so great because the bachelor had no wife with whom the injured husband could reciprocate.

The maintenance of discipline within each family was strictly a family affair, and the Chickahominy did not spare the rod in their dealings with children. Any youngster who violated the taboos of the nation was whipped, fathers beating their sons and mothers attending to the punishment of their daughters. In all probability Pocahontas was never spanked. Her father was forbidden by custom to lay hands on her, and only her mother could have taken the rod to her; since she was the direct descendant of the Chief of Chiefs, it is unlikely that Powhatan's sisters, possessing royal blood themselves, would have dared to touch her.

Even though the functions of the Council were few, the body met regularly, usually assembling on the day following the appearance of a new moon. Either the chief or the Bi-tan could summon the Council to a meeting at any time these leaders believed a session was warranted. The decisions of the group were binding on the entire nation, and

15

were enforced by the senior warriors. These braves were the backbone of the army in time of war and made up an informal but highly effective constabulary in peacetime. In fact, most quarrels were settled by senior warriors, acting on their own authority.

When a warrior had lived fifty summers, he retired from the active life of the Chickahominy, moving to a long house for elders and thereafter enjoying leisure until he died. The elders, who were supported by the entire community, hunted and fished at will, but were not required to depend on their own efforts for their food. They drowsed in the sun, received regular visits of homage paid by their children and grandchildren, and were venerated by the entire society. Soon each of them would be joining the family's deified original ancestor, and therefore was a man to be treated with great respect.

The younger wife of a man who moved to the long house of elders was presumed to be a widow from that time forward, and had the right to marry any man of her own choice, a privilege denied unwedded girls, whose husbands were chosen for them by their fathers and brothers. In some ways the old women of the Chickahominy were regarded as menials and enjoyed few benefits. They were required to work in the fields until they were sixty summers old, and thereafter they continued to cook for themselves and their unmarried offspring. At sixty they were entitled to enter an elders' lodge of their own and be supported by the community.

In spite of its surface appearances, however, the Chickahominy society was essentially a matriarchy. The wife and mother was the hardworking core of the family, and most decisions were made by her. In theory the warrior who hunted and went off to battle was all-powerful, and consequently could not be bothered with the petty problems of daily living. In fact, the squaws took advantage of this situation and gathered the reins of power into their own hands, rarely referring any matter to their husbands, who were essentially lazy.

The squaws inflicted punishment on cowards and bachelors who had affairs with married women, the adulterous wife never being punished for her transgressions.

The squaws tortured prisoners of war until these unfortunates agreed to change sides and swear fealty in blood to the Chickahominy. The squaws drove a thief into the wilderness after stripping him of his weapons, and beat him without mercy if he dared to show his face again in any town or village of the Chickahominy.

Sloth had made the warriors such an indifferent lot that the women held their husbands in great contempt, saved the best cuts of meat and the finest fruits and vegetables for themselves and their daughters, and rejoiced when they gave birth to girl children. For more than three hundred and fifty years students of the life of Pocahontas have wondered why it was so easy for her to abandon her own people and marry an English settler. The answer is as obvious as the explanation provided by Lady de la Warr: she admired the energy and ambition of the settler, and shared the contempt of other Chickahominy women for the warriors of her own nation. Even her own father, although regarded with awe by most of his people, was no hero to his daughter, who was disgusted by his idleness.

The women, to be sure, were as responsible as the men for the attitudes developed by their sons, although they may not have realized it. A boy could not be beaten by his mother, but she could prod him with a sharpened stick when she wished, and she joined her husband in teaching him certain values, almost from birth. Like many other Indian nations, the Chickahominy considered stoicism a male virtue, and from the earliest age boys were taught to endure physical and mental suffering, fatigue and privation. A boy was expected to be a swift runner, to handle a spear, a bow and arrow or a stone-bladed ax with expertise; he was also expected to endure pain without complaint, and it was enough that he learned to live up to this ideal. Certainly he could not lower his male dignity by working in the fields, cooking the family's meals or making clothing.

One of the fascinations of Pocahontas's childhood is that, as the daughter of the Chief of Chiefs, her upbringing was unique. From the time of her birth it was taken for granted that she would marry a son of the Bi-tan, one of her distant cousins, and this assumption was based on practical considerations. Unlike the princesses of Great Britain, the Continent or the Near East, whose husbands were chosen for them abroad in order to form and cement political alliances, Pocahontas would marry within the ranks of the Chickahominy, as did all other women of the nation. A tribe was proud of its heritage, regarding all others as foreigners, and it was unthinkable that a princess of the Chickahominy would follow an alien husband to the land of his birth. Equally important, the daughter of the Chief of Chiefs would not be expected to plant, tend and harvest crops, cook meals or cut and sew animal skins, tasks that were beneath the dignity of royalty. Her aunts were attended by servants, perhaps slaves who had been captured from other tribes and impressed into domestic service, and she would have her own retinue, too.

So the only man Pocahontas could marry would be the son of a Bi-tan. His other wives would perform the necessary household functions while she remained serene and isolated, directing their activities. But the Chickahominy, being close to nature, were a realistic people, and they knew that unless a princess received a thorough education her inferiors might be able to take advantage of her. Consequently she went into the fields to grow crops, spent hours at the pits were meals were cooked over heated stones and learned to use a bone needle and leather-cutting knife.

She was also permitted to engage in many of the activities customarily reserved for young braves, and this phase of Pocahontas's education was documented by Captain Samuel Argall, the man who abducted her from the Chickahominy. Rationalizing the kidnapping, he explained to the Governor and Council of Jamestown that she was "as expert in the art of making war as any savage brave." Certainly it was true that she learned to throw an ax and shoot an arrow with deadly accuracy. As an adult she paid a visit to the country house of King James I at Hampton Court Palace, and astonished members of the royal entourage there with demonstrations of her prowess.

Her indulgence in athletic activities kept her slender. As a young woman she had narrow hips, a tiny waist and small, high breasts, a figure that was anything but fashionable in her own time but more nearly resembled the ideal of the latter portion of the twentieth century. She developed great stamina as a runner, and the ordeal she endured with dignity and calm after her abduction by Argall—as will be seen hints she well might have learned the stoicism the Chickahominy usually taught only to young males.

It is difficult to believe, however, that as a part of her training she was sent out into the forest alone for days at a time, armed only with a small knife fashioned of the iron found near the Tumbling Water of the Great River, later to be known as the Falls of the James River, the site of present-day Richmond, Virginia. It is unlikely she was forced to go without food and water for days on end in order to strengthen her spirit, and it is inconceivable that the daughter of the Chief of Chiefs was made to endure torture that toughened the skins and resolve of young Chickahominy warriors. Whatever her training, however, she absorbed it well and stood up to the test in her time of trial.

As a member of royalty Pocahontas was subject to no authority except her father's and, to a limited degree, that of the elder of her brothers, Mataoko, whose name meant "first born son." The inability of others to instill discipline caused her to run wild as a small child, and she was fortunate she did not grow into a badly spoiled young woman. For a portion of his daughter's childhood, perhaps as long as three or four years, Powhatan was preoccupied with matters of state, and during that time Pocahontas's activities were virtually unsupervised. It was then that she most frequently dressed like a boy, went hunting and fishing with Piaoko and his friends, climbed trees and otherwise behaved in a manner unbecoming to a princess. Even if the Chief of Chiefs had authorized his sisters to discipline the girl as they saw fit, it is improbable that the most courageous of squaws would have dared to beat Pocahontas very hard. She was her father's favorite and in his eyes could do little wrong.

When Powhatan had an opportunity to pay close attention to his daughter again, he appears to have been appalled by what he saw. How he chose to teach her discipline is not known, but whatever his methods may have been, Matoaka, whose name meant "first born daughter," became far more circumspect, dressed in a young squaw's attire and gave up her hunting trips.

She was still enough of a tomboy, however, to startle and shock the hard-bitten Englishmen of Jamestown in 1611, four years after the founding of the colony, when she accompanied her father and brothers there on what can best be described as a visit of state. According to the written accounts and diaries of several colonists, which agree on essentials, she climbed trees, did somersaults and performed acrobatics, and early one morning was found shinnying up the steeple of the uncompleted Jamestown church.

According to Robert Ker, Earl of Somerset, for many years the favorite of King James I, Pocahontas told him one of her favorite pastimes had been playing a boy's game vaguely like modern soccer. A ball made of tightly woven vines was kicked forward or passed laterally to one's teammates as they drove toward their opponents' goal, and players could utilize any means at their disposal to thwart the drive of their foes. Jamestown colonists who saw the game played, and were stunned by its ferocity, wrote that players tackled, bit, gouged, clawed and kicked one another with happy abandon. If Pocahontas actually played the game, she could expect no easy treatment from opponents because she was a girl or a princess. It was not unusual for players to be badly injured or maimed, and several Jamestown colonists wrote that players subjected to concerted attacks by their foes sometimes died of injuries sustained on the field. The game was encouraged by senior braves because it toughened future warriors, and Pocahontas must have suffered her fair share of blows and kicks.

She did not yet realize it, but she was undergoing preparations for extraordinary adventures and a life unlike that led by any other Chickahominy in the nation's long history.

III

Most of the Indian nations of the Atlantic seaboard of North America were nature worshippers, deifying the sun, the moon, the wind and even the forests in which they made their homes and eked out a marginal existence. The Chickahominy, however, more nearly resembled the tribes of the Great Plains, and in some aspects of their religious customs were like the nations of what are now Oregon and Washington. To date, no definitive explanation for the passage of these customs for a distance of three thousand overland miles has ever been offered.

A huge stone pit stood at one end of the main

Chickahominy town, and the thick cluster of pines that encircled it cut it off from the view of inhabitants and visitors. According to several Jamestown travelers, a platform made of light, dried wood was built over the pit. When a man died, he and his belongings were placed on the platform, a huge fire was made in the pit below, an the dead man was cremated. Whenever a platform burned to the ground, another rose to take its place. Prayers were recited by the Bi-tan and his assistants during the funeral service, commending the departed to the care of his first ancestor, and within twenty-four hours another platform was constructed, members of the Chickahominy superstitiously believing that a failure to replace the platform with another would be the worst of bad luck. Squaws who died were also cremated, but no religious ceremony was performed for them, and only a simple service was held for males under twenty-five summers of age.

Pocahontas was proud of her ancestors, speaking of them with great dignity in London many years after she last witnessed a Chickahominy funeral in the wilderness where her forebears had lived and died. But the faith of the Indian nation was far too simple and basic for the daughter of Powhatan, and neither the Bi-tan nor his assistants knew the answers to the many questions that went through the girl's mind. How did the Chickahominy *know* their gods were their own ancestors? How did these deities make themselves and their works identifiable? At what moment did the soul of one's ancestor enter the physical being of an infant, how did the soul function and why was its presence necessary if one hoped to attain happiness and success?

The theology of the Chickahominy being relatively limited, the Bi-tan must have been disconcerted, to say the least, when the inquiring Pocahontas hurled her queries at him and reacted with anger when he tried to side-step. The religion the Chickahominy had accepted for generations was being jeopardized by a girl who asked what no one else had wanted to know. So it is small wonder that, as a young woman, Pocahontas eagerly accepted another ancient faith as one that better met her personal needs.

The traditions of the Chickahominy were exclusively

oral, the nation having no written language, so the Bi-tan and his assistants committed to memory the prayers to ancestors that were chanted for the dead, for the newborn, for the braves who went off to war and for a plentiful harvest, as well as other, special prayers for occasions the Chickahominy regarded as minor. The daughter of a great chieftain was required to know things beyond the ken of other squaws, so Pocahontas was required to memorize these prayers, too.

Many years later, at Whitehall, she recited and translated them for some of the scholars who had just finished the monumental task of translating the King James Bible from the original Hebrew and Greek. One of them, Bishop John Trelawny of Cornwall, subsequently wrote that the performance had left a deep impression on him. The religion of the Indians was "beautiful in its simplicity," he declared, and "although frankly pagan in its conceptualization, might be regarded as a savage Christianity, lacking the essential figure of Christ." Later theologians have spent more than three hundred years trying to understand what the good Bishop may have thought he meant.

The Chickahominy were not a religious people in the Judeo-Christian meaning of the word. Their faith was ceremonial, and was not applied to their day-to-day lives; a man's conduct on earth in no way related to his union with his original ancestor when he died. That meeting was guaranteed regardless of how he behaved, and he was punished in life for his misdemeanors.

As previously noted, that punishment was social, as a general rule, and usually consisted of ostracization. Under no circumstances would a Chickahominy be killed by his fellow countrymen as a punishment, and the worst that could happen to him was banishment from the tribe, which was a virtual guarantee of slow death. Prisons were unknown to the nation, as they were to most North American Indians, and those who transgressed the taboos of the Chickahominy were punished without delay.

One of the most vicious punishments was also used to test the mettle of young warriors and was always utilized in the treatment of enemy braves captured in battle. The victim was required to run the gauntlet, passing between a double line of men armed with sticks, knives and clubs, who maimed him and beat him unconscious if he failed to make his way from the beginning of the line to the end. Then he was handed over to the women for more refined tortures, and it was not uncommon for the poor victim to spend several agonizing days tied to a stake, where he was subjected to varieties of ill treatment before being released.

A more subtle and excruciating punishment was meted out to cowards and to bachelors who had the temerity to sleep with married women. These unfortunates were handed over to the squaws, and for the rest of their lives were treated as females. Their eyebrows were plucked, they wore their hair long, their lips were stained and they wore women's attire. They were compelled to labor in the fields each day, and when they returned to the town of the Chickahominy at night, they were used as prostitutes by the bachelors of the community, the incidence of homosexuality among the Chickahominy being high, as it was in many tribes.

It was regarded as far more degrading to make such a person the lifelong plaything and sex object of men. A number of Jamestown settlers noted that most of these creatures became gentle and placid, and even when offered the opportunity to leave the land of the Chickahominy preferred to retain female attire, pose as women and engage in sexual relations only with men. Their spirits were broken and they were totally corrupted by the treatment they received.

Very few Chickahominy were punished for violations of the nation's taboos, the tribe being too easygoing to demand strict observance of any but the basic rules that governed their society. It has been estimated that the tribe achieved its population peak under the rule of Powhatan, when it may have numbered as many as five thousand to six thousand members, and only a handful were ever punished at any given time for breaking the law. Certainly it is doubtful that Pocahontas saw anything of these violators. She would not have been considered too delicate to be exposed to them, but there would have been no reason for her, as one of the aristocrats of the nation, to deal with them in any way. She had more than enough to keep her busy.

It was thanks almost exclusively to her, after she had

lived in Jamestown for a time and had married there, that a supposedly more sophisticated society learned that Indian diets were neither simple nor monotonous. Traditional myth has insisted that dishes prepared by the Indians were crude, consisting in the main of roasted or jerked meats, smoked fish and cornmeal paste, but Pocahontas taught the English that the Chickahominy could prepare many delightful dishes, which the settlers quickly claimed as their own.

Although Pocahontas, by her own admission at the court of King James, was not an accomplished cook, she nevertheless made a number of significant contributions to the gastronomy of her adopted world. One of the most popular, which is prepared with variations down to the present day, has been popular since her own time. Oysters were opened, sprinkled with crumbs of cornmeal, then edible seaweed that had been soaked in a solution of garlic and water was placed over the top, and the half-shells were baked on hot rocks. Equally attractive was the dressing of cornmeal and various herbs used as the stuffing for roasted or baked fowl.

Soups, as such, were virtually unknown to the Chickahominy, but every squaw knew how to prepare a stew of the tougher cuts of venison or bear, which simmered for hours with chunks of root vegetables. Iron cooking pots were unknown to the Chickahominy and other Indian nations of the New World during Pocahontas's childhood, such utensils being introduced by the Jamestown settlers, who offered them in barter. Most cooking was done in very heavy, thick clay pots and pans which had been baked very slowly over low fires to make them strong. In spite of these precautions, however, most Chickahominy pots were fragile, so foods other than roasts were always cooked over small fires. Squaws frequently needed three or four hours to prepare the principal meal of the day, but patience was a virtue the Indians cultivated from early childhood, and no one objected.

The Chickahominy ate only two meals each day, and when the strangers came to the New World in their large ships, bringing with them Old World eating habits, they were regarded by the natives as gluttons. The squaws worked in the fields for at least an hour or two every morning before returning to the town to prepare breakfast, and as their time

25

was valuable to them, the first meal of the day was simple and could be prepared quickly. A typical breakfast consisted of grilled fish and a flat bread of coarsely ground cornmeal that had been baked the previous night. A beverage made of boiled acorns, to which herbs were sometimes added, was served in hollow gourds. No one except small children ate again until evening.

When hunters killed a deer, bear or wild boar, they were responsible for roasting it over the cooking pit, as the process took hours and the women would not return from the fields until sundown. On ordinary occasions the evening meal was not served until long after nightfall, and invariably consisted of a single course that included meat and whatever wild vegetables might be available. Corn was cultivated, the women using fish as fertilizer, and large quantities of corn bread usually were available, except in times of great shortage. Sometimes finely chopped nuts were added to the bread, which could be preserved for long periods in this way, and warriors took quantitites of it with them on prolonged hunting trips and military expeditions.

The storage bins of the Chickahominy were filled with smoked meats and salted fish, and every family was required to contribute a fair share during the spring, summer and early autumn. Then, when winter came, each could take what it required from the common store. The threat of being denied the privilege of taking food from the common store kept every hunter and fisherman busy during the warmer seasons. All grain cultivated by the women and all fruits, vegetables and nuts that were gathered went straight into the communal bins. If one family ate, all ate; if one went hungry, all went hungry.

Fruits were almost never eaten raw, the Chickahominy having learned they could be preserved indefinitely by boiling them and storing them, in sealed clay pots, in their own syrup. They were usually served during the winter months, when fresh vegetables became scarce.

Desserts were a rarity in the diets of the Chickahominy, but Pocahontas, even as an adult, was fond of a children's treat, little cakes of chopped nuts held together with wild honey. The dish was prepared in London according to her recipe, but she declared it inferior to the Chickahominy product, saying it retained its full flavor only when the honey was wild.

Families ate their meals together, the warrior and his squaw squatting on one side of the fire, their children ranging along the far side. Meat was served in chunks, and was held, smoking hot, in the right hand, with the diner biting off pieces as he consumed the whole strip. Other dishes were usually served in individual gourds, which the squaw dipped into her cooking pot. Adult males were served first, then the squaws served themselves, and the children were served in accordance with their seniority. Children who had gone off to the long houses usually returned to the homes of their parents for their evening meals, but were required to contribute to the larder, the girls being given a quota in the fields, the boys being directed to bring in quantities of game, fowl and fish.

It is unlikely that Pocahontas was given a set quota, the family of the Chief of Chiefs being exempted, but her brothers felt it was their duty to set an example for the other warriors by bringing home more meat and fish than anyone else. So it is likely that the girl did more than her fair share, too. And if she shot and snared animals instead of cultivating corn with the other women, no one was in a position to protest. Meat, as every Chickahominy knew, was more important than grain.

The only eating utensil used by the Chickahominy was a flint knife attached to a long handle of bone or wood with a leather thong. Meat could be either cut or speared with it, and the expert could wield such a knife with great delicacy. Many drawings were made of the Chickahominy knife that Pocahontas gave as a gift to her good friend Anne of Denmark, the wife of King James I. The utensil was kept at the royal court for many years, and was exhibited there as a curiosity, but was either lost or stolen during the civil war that cost Charles I, the son of James and Anne, his throne and his head. The knife was never recovered.

The Chickahominy celebrated no established feast days or other holidays, probably because they never knew from one year to the next whether they would be enjoying a glut of food or suffering near starvation. During years of plenty, however, it was customary to hold impromptu celebrations, to which the leaders of other tribes in what would become Virginia and Delaware were invited. Even on these occasions, it must be emphasized, hosts and guests ate sparingly. American Indians appreciated well-cooked food, as have virtually all other people throughout human history, but it was rare to find a gourmand in their ranks. They remained lean because meat and fish formed the principal staples of their diet, and although they leaned heavily on corn, they failed to realize the full potential of the grain, using it only as meal that they made into unleavened bread.

Captain John Smith, the leader of the Jamestown colony during its most critical period and the author of two exceptionally popular books about his experiences in the New World, indicated in some of his writing that the Chickahominy drank a brew of fermented corn. But he was mistaken, as he was in so much he wrote about the Indians, and it must be presumed that he simply found it difficult to imagine any people living without alcoholic beverages. The truth of the matter is that the Chickahominy, like all other Indian nations of North America, were unfamiliar with the processes of fermentation and distillation, and alcoholic beverages were unknown to them.

Pocahontas was introduced to ale and wine for the first time during her sojourn in Jamestown, and cordially detested both. Later, in England, she found it necessary to take ceremonial sips of wine at state dinners and other functions when toasts were offered, but she never developed a palate for even the mildest of wines.

Milk was unknown to the Chickahominy, too, and none was available in Jamestown, either, so Pocahontas probably never tasted either milk or cream until she reached England.

Like all members of her nation, she undoubtedly drank large quantities of water. Early settlers in Virginia, Massachusetts Bay and elsewhere in the New World were astonished by the amounts of water the natives of the continent consumed. This was particularly surprising because most Indian foods were unsalted; in fact, only fish was salted, after being smoked, in order to preserve it for fairly long periods.

It is unlikely that Pocahontas developed a taste for fish. The Chickahominy of the interior were meat eaters, although they caught fish in their rivers, and also obtained quantities of shellfish from their villages on Chesapeake Bay, in barter for venison, bear, wild boar and other game. But they ate fish only in times of emergency, when their supplies of meat were practically exhausted. The braves of the Chickahominy interior would eat fish only when no other food was available, regarding it as a squaw's dish. The women were more broad-minded, and having discovered that fish could be a delicacy when properly prepared, they were less reluctant to eat it. But at no time was it popular with any but those branches of the nation that lived on the shores of Chesapeake Bay or the open Atlantic Ocean.

Pocahontas, like all of the Chickahominy, remained slender because she subsisted on a diet of unsalted meat, root vegetables and fruit, washed down with water. Her food obviously agreed with her, and she is not known to have suffered a single day of illness until she moved to a different world and succumbed to the ailment that proved fatal.

Unlike many other nations, the Chickahominy had no "medicine men" or other healers. When someone fell ill, he was given various herbs by elderly squaws who had learned the recipes from their mothers. When an ailment proved serious, the sufferer was moved to an isolated hut, and there he either recovered on his own or died in lonely dignity. Disease was almost unknown to the Chickahominy and other Indian tribes until the English, French and Spaniards came to the New World, so it is probable that Pocahontas took her good health for granted.

IV

Chickahominy adults enjoyed a simple, ordered life, but the same was not the case for their children, members of the nation long having known that it was necessary to instill discipline in the young at an early age. It was customary to begin active training as soon as a baby could walk and talk.

The childhood of Pocahontas was even more complicated than that of other Chickahominy children, in part because she had no mother, and partly, of course, because of her father's exalted position. It has been assumed that the first seven years of her life were spent with at least two of Powhatan's sisters, both of them widows, and that she lived

with them in a one-room hut in the large dwelling and
working compound of the Chief of Chiefs. The ground was
the floor of this crude building. There were no windows and a
flap of animal skins was lowered over the entrance for privacy.
Made of clay, mud and sticks, the building protected the
inhabitants from some of winter's cold, but it must have been
stifling in summer.

The little girl slept on a bed of tender pine boughs, over
which an animal skin may have been spread, and as she knew
no other kind of sleeping couch, she probably found the
accommodations comfortable. Most Indian tribes were
unsanitary, so body lice were common, but the
Chickahominy were an exception, and followed the practice
of changing their pine boughs at regular, frequent intervals.
The women were responsible for gathering the boughs, so
Pocahontas must have been taken into the forests by her aunts
at a very early age. There she helped them cut and collect the
new beds, and was taught to distinguish between young
boughs and those of hard, gnarled wood.

During the warmer months, perhaps sixty percent of
each year, the child was totally unclad. The sun and wind
toned her skin, and the soles of her feet became hard, enabling
her to walk on rocks, pebbles and shells without discomfort.
Since all other little girls and boys also went naked, she took
her nudity for granted and was in no way self-conscious.

In the colder weather she was clad in a single garment,
probably a knee-length dress made of sewn animal skins,
sleeveless and loose-fitting. On the few days when the winter
weather became bitter, she donned a cape made of the fur of
the fox, the wolf or the rabbit. But only when the ground
became hard underfoot, in mid-winter, was she permitted to
wear crudely-cut moccasins. Some children rarely bothered
and hated all footgear.

It is worthy of note that the Chickahominy, unlike the
tribes who lived farther north, did not smear their skins in
winter with a protective coating of animal fat. Emissaries from
the nations of the north sometimes came to the land of
Chickahominy for visits, so the practice must have been
known, but the weather was mild enough to make the habit

unnecessary. This lack of grease inadvertantly contributed to the cleanliness of the tribe.

The location of the town on the banks of what would become known as the James River was of great importance to every Chickahominy child as well as to the nation's adults. Not only was drinking water plentiful, but all members of the tribe swam regularly. Men and women bathed together, shedding their few items of clothing before plunging into the water, and from earliest childhood, even before she could walk, Pocahontas paddled in the shallows near the grassy bank.

As an adult living in England she remarked to Queen Anne, who was fascinated by the information, that she could not remember a time when she had been unable to swim. Whether she was actually taught is unknown, but it is improbable she received lessons. If she followed the usual Chickahominy practice, she simply followed the example of older children and progressed rapidly from a paddler to a real swimmer.

Small children traditionally were treated with greater leniency when they left the confines of the town, in part because they came to terms with the wilderness at a tender age. A girl who cut herself on a thorn would treat a bush with greater respect the next time she brushed against one, and a child who stepped into a trap set for small game by the older boys would become wary. Girls and boys roamed through the forest at will on berry-gathering expeditions, and it was on these occasions that Pocahontas soon proved she was the daughter of the Chief of Chiefs. She preferred the company of boys to girls, she quickly learned to climb higher in the trees than any of her contemporaries, and she later revealed that no one could beat her in a foot race.

But she could not flout all of the nation's traditions, and certain activities were denied her because of her sex. A little boy began to handle a throwing ax, a spear and a bow and arrow before he passed his fourth summer, but little girls were not allowed to use the weapons of the hunt and of war.

In some mysterious way she managed to learn more than the adults realized, however, and according to an educated guess she was taught surreptitiously by the younger of her brothers, Piaoko, who may have been approximately four or five years her senior. However she may have acquired the skill, she was sufficiently adept to go on hunting trips with Piaoko when she was about ten. According to a story that subsequently gained credence in Jamestown, she was approximately twelve when she brought down a wild boar, and was in the process of cutting out her arrow when her father and a party of warriors arrived at the scene. A wild boar was a dangerous beast when cornered, and could seriously injure the unwary, but Powhatan was so delighted when he discovered his daughter's prowess that, thereafter, he occasionally bent the traditions of the nation and permitted her to accompany him on hunting expeditions.

All who encountered Pocahontas in Jamestown, and later in London, commented at length on the beauty of her carriage. She walked with her head held high, her back straight and her shoulders squared. Her stride was long and effortless, and she seemed to glide rather than walk. This was not accidental. Like all Chickahominy girls, she was taught how to walk, and there can be little doubt that her aunts, like other women of the nation, kept birch whips in their hut for purposes of aiding and speeding instruction. The sting of a lash on one's bare calves, buttocks or back quickly taught a small girl the error of her ways and helped her to learn the approved manner of walking in the shortest possible time.

The Chickahominy could neither read nor write, and were less advanced than a number of other tribes in picture writing. But the history and traditions of the nation were preserved from generation to generation in song and legend, and Pocahontas received instructions from the time she was two or three years old. Other children of the tribe struggled endlessly to remember the legends of their ancestors, but the memory of the little princess was so phenomenal that, when she paid her first visit to Jamestown in her early teens, she astonished her English hosts by declaiming at length without fault or prompting.

The friendship of the Chickahominy and the English settlers cooled rapidly after Pocahontas's time, and within a generation the tribe was dispersed. So posterity is permanently in the debt of the young woman who, more than any other single person, was responsible for the making of a permanent record of Chickahominy history and customs.

It is necessary to read between the lines to discover that Pocahontas cared nothing for the company of other girls and avoided them when possible. At no time in her later life did she mention any close friendships with other members of her own sex. Boys, including those of her own age and Piaoko's friends, who were somewhat older, were her constant, chosen companions. She competed with them in swimming and in foot races, and only when they engaged in trials of strength and endurance that prepared them for their later lives as warriors was she excluded.

It is impossible to draw even an approximate portrait of Pocahontas in her early years. By present-day standards she was not spoiled, but she went far beyond the boundaries the Chickahominy set for their children, and no one but the favorite daughter of the great Powhatan would have been treated so permissively. Due to her exceptional intelligence she did not lose her perspective, however, and her disposition was so cheerful she offended neither adults nor members of her own generation. It is easy to imagine, though, that girls of her own age were jealous of her.

Posterity has been given no verifiable accounts of Pocahontas's early years, and most of the stories of her childhood that have survived are probably apocryphal. Even if they are suspect, however, they lend a flavor to the life of a child of the Chickahominy nation in her era.

One tale that is still repeated concerns an alleged occasion when Pocahontas, then about six years of age, went fishing in the river with several boys, presumably Piaoko and several of his friends. The youngsters cast bits of bait onto the surface near deep pools in the river, then speared the fish that rose for the food. The boys made several attempts to catch one particularly large, agile fish, but failed, and then Pocahontas is alleged to have speared it in a single thrust. It is unlikely, of course, that a small girl of six, whose experience in the handling of a stone-tipped spear was necessarily far more limited than that of boys who were ten or eleven, would have succeeded where they had failed. But the story does indicate that the children of the Chickahominy went fishing with spears, and it may be true that Pocahontas accompanied groups of boys on their outings.

According to another story, she showed such proficiency with languages from earliest childhood that she became her father's official interpreter at a very young age. This account should be taken with a large chunk of salt from the deer licks on the heights above the James River. While it is true that the girl proved herself astonishingly adept in her ability to learn English at the appropriate time, there was never a need for her to act as an interpreter for her father. The differences in the dialects of the tribes of the area were slight, but their basic tongues were approximately the same, so Powhatan and a visitor from another Indian nation could understand each other without the services of an interpreter.

There may be some truth in yet another of the Pocahontas legends. For the better part of two centuries after her time it was said that a large rock that towered above a bend in the James River was the site of a dramatic incident. According to this story, Pocahontas ran away to Jamestown when in her early teens, was recognized by settlers who had visited the Chickahominy and was handed over to a searching party led by the elder of her brothers, Mataoko. She was returned to her family in disgrace, and Powhatan, who held court on the rock, forgave his daughter when she smiled at him but proudly refused to plead for mercy and forgiveness.

It may be true, as will be seen later, that Pocahontas did run away from the land of the Chickahominy and make an appearance at Jamestown, since she displayed an exceptionally lively curiosity about the English settlement from the beginning. If she did show up there, the settlers would have been quick to return her to her own people, fearing her father's wrath if they detained her. But the rest of the tale must be pure fiction. The standards of the Chickahominy were not those of the men from the far side of the Atlantic, and as Powhatan proved on a far more important and dramatic occasion some years later, a daughter who disappeared from home was expected to take the consequences. So it is improbable that any scene of forgiveness and reconciliation took place at the great rock or anywhere else.

Only a final word need be said about Pocahontas's earliest years. The hair of all Chickahominy children was allowed to grow long until a youngster's seventh summer. At that age the hair of boys was shaved, with a scalp-lock left in the center, running back across the crown of his head. The hair of a girl was arranged for the first time in a thick, single braid, and she wore it in that style until puberty. This custom was inviolable, so it is safe to assume that in 1602, as the strangers who would come to the New World recorded the passage of time, Pocahontas's hair was braided as a symbol of a new phase in her life. At no time was her hair ever cut, and eventually it fell in a thick, blue-black wave to her hips. At the age of seven she probably realized only that it was a relief not to have masses of it falling in her face when she ran or swam or went out into the forest.

By this time Pocahontas probably began to resemble the young woman who would create such a stir when she went to England. According to various contemporary accounts, she had clear, large eyes with long lashes and thin lids, a straight nose that was shorter than that of most Indians, typically high cheekbones, a firm chin and full, well-formed lips. Unfortunately, her precise appearance at any age must remain a matter of conjecture.

Scores of portraits and drawings have been made of her over the centuries, many claiming to be "authentic," but without exception they are the idealized works of artists who never saw her. No drawings were made of her in Jamestown during her adolescence or thereafter, and, as will be seen, the only man talented enough to make even a sketch of her, Captain John Smith, was at no time in a position to do so.

It has been alleged that the Chickahominy princess sat for a number of painters during her London sojourn, which is a reasonable assumption, but no known portraits by British artists of the period have ever been found. Scores of hoaxes have been painted subsequently, but it has been impossible to prove that any is genuine.

Certainly no precise word portrait of the seven-year-old

Pocahontas can be drawn, and it is unlikely that she herself would have recognized her resemblance. Mirrors were unknown in the land of the Chickahominy, and at most the little girl would have caught a glimpse of her reflection in the clear waters of the river or in a forest pond. Indian women had little chance to indulge their vanity, and growing girls had even fewer opportunities. Besides, Pocahontas was probably too busy in the years that stretched ahead to think much about herself.

V

Wearing clothes for the first time in her young life, the seven-year-old Pocahontas found herself thrust, overnight, into a world of responsibility. If the custom of her people was followed, as was probable, she made her first dress of animal skins herself, cutting and sewing the strips of leather under the guidance of her aunts. As the daughter of the tribe's leader she was entitled to wear attire adorned with shells stained with vegetable dyes, but the patterns made with the shells was intricate, so this work may have been done on her behalf by her aunts.

Now that she was seven, no male, her father included,

was permitted to administer corporal punishment. It is not known whether Powhatan switched her during her earlier years, but henceforth he was not allowed to raise a hand to her in either anger or chastisement. In fact, the taboos of the Chickahominy prevented a male of any age from having physical contact with her.

According to one of the mistaken myths of early Americana, the Indians were undemonstrative people who went to great lengths in order to avoid showing emotions. This impression is totally false. Most nations, the Chickahominy included, were warm, light-hearted people who made little or no attempt to conceal their feelings with their own, and assumed a stoical, wooden facade only in the presence of outsiders. But one rule that not even Pocahontas would have been permitted to break was that which strictly forbade physical contact with members of the opposite sex, beginning at the age of seven.

Pocahontas is portrayed by innumerable artists in the act of throwing herself onto her father as she pleads for the life of John Smith, a pose which illustrates the dramatic story that is the core of the Pocahontas legend. The artists were not exercising their own imaginations, but were merely illustrating the detailed story told by Smith himself. Anyone familiar with the history and custom of the Chickahominy, however, knows that this could not have happened. Not even the most tender-hearted of girls would have dared to violate one of the fundamental taboos of her people by having physical contact with her father.

It is probable, however, that the little girl and her aunts exchanged frequent gestures of affection. As an adolescent and as a woman Pocahontas showed no sign of having been denied love in her earlier days, and everyone who knew her commented on her spontaneously warm and loving nature. Her sense of humor was highly developed, too, and she often laughed aloud, so it is safe to say that as a child she did her share of giggling.

The Chickahominy, like so many primitive people, enjoyed nothing more than a practical joke, and the boys and girls of pre-puberty age had ample opportunities to play tricks on each other. Small parties of these children were sent into the forest together, usually under the guidance of a junior warrior; the boys were expected to hunt small game, which the girls then butchered and dressed, these activities obviously preparing them for their future vocations.

A favorite trick played by the boys on these occasions was that of digging a hole in the ground, covering it with a network of sticks and brush and then enticing a girl to fall into the trap. Although Pocahontas was the daughter of the nation's leader, her person was in no way sancrosanct, so she was forced to endure the indignity of dropping into a pit on a number of occasions.

She retaliated against her tormentors in the approved manner. The girls were expected to prepare the meals on these expeditions, and she learned from those who were older how to obtain revenge. A wise girl surreptitiously gathered certain roots and plants, which she cooked with the boys' meals and then discarded before they could be detected. Some made a boy's food bitter to the taste, but he could not admit having been tricked without losing face, so he was compelled to eat his meal, even though tears came to his eyes. An even more subtle instrument of revenge was an innocent-looking yellow blossom that shriveled and disappeared when cooked, and that caused violent diarrhea.

From the age of seven, boys spent increasingly long hours in the wilderness, learning to hunt, familiarizing themselves with the forest and developing the physical stamina and endurance that was essential to every brave. They were taught to make and use their own weapons, and they practiced by the hour, it being a difficult feat to throw a crude ax or shoot a hand-shaped arrow with any degree of accuracy.

The girls were equally busy. Each was given her own small plot of ground, which was made larger each year, and by the time she was ten she was expected to grow all of her own corn. In years when the weather was favorable and the crop was ample, a girl who had been careless or lazy and grew less than was expected was given no other corn to eat. Pocahontas was not exempted from this rule, but she found work in the fields boring and it did not take her long to discover and develop shortcuts that enabled her to spend less time tending her plot.

She and Piaoko still enjoyed a close relationship, and the boy, later recognized by the Jamestown settlers as an exceptionally talented fisherman and hunter, often took his sister with him on his excursions. Pocahontas became expert in the art of spearing fish, but she would have been reprimanded by her aunts had they known she had gone off to enjoy herself when she should have been working, so she had to dispose of her catch before being apprehended. Cleverly, she buried the fish in her plot of ground, which became the most richly fertilized in the entire community.

Her corn grew taller than any other, and it was agreed that the daughter of Powhatan had a touch of her own as a farmer. Pocahontas would remember the tricks of her childhood in her later years, when her husband became the first to grow tobacco in Virginia, and her contribution was at least partly responsible for his extraordinary success. As has already been seen, the use of fish as fertilizer long had been a practice of the Chickahominy, but Pocahontas, as a mischievous little girl, increased the quantity of fish for her own purposes, and inadvertantly enriched the soil even more.

The girl also expended much time and effort at the cooking pits, an activity she disliked even more than she did working in the fields. In spite of her feelings, however, she became a fairly accomplished cook, which stood her in good stead when she became a housewife in Jamestown, a community in which servants were lacking, although she ultimately had two.

In one feminine sphere Pocahontas developed a genuine interest, and her talent grew rapidly, too. She proved to be exceptionally clever with a needle and knife, and soon was making not only her own clothes but those of other members of the family. It was no accident in later years that she acquired a reputation as one of the most handsomely dressed women in fashionable London, where people were stunned by the instinct she displayed for wearing the right clothes at the right time.

Some time after her seventh year Pocahontas's

relationship with the elder of her brothers, Mataoko, gained depth and solidity. The future Chief of Chiefs was at least a decade older than his little sister, and having been required to demonstrate his skills and endurance at an earlier age than most Chickahominy males, had already achieved the status of a senior warrior. He was a member of his father's Council, of course, and in preparation for his future role as the leader of a confederation of nations, he had paid prolonged visits to the other tribes that would come under his rule.

Mataoko, who subsequently conducted most of his father's business with the Jamestown settlers, became a familiar figure in the English colony, and a number of the leaders there wrote about him at some length. Lord de la Warr, probably the best of Jamestown's administrators, described Mataoko as a shrewd bargainer, a man of great dignity who was scrupulously honest and always kept his word, and a man ever-conscious of the traditions of his people. He was six feet tall, a giant in an age when most men were several inches shorter than they are in the twentieth century. Lady de la Warr thought he looked like the Earl of Southampton, who was considered devastating by most English ladies of the period. All of Powhatan's children, it appears, were handsome.

A man of grave demeanor who was conscious of his high estate and of the problems he would face when he inherited his father's throne, Mataoko was irritated by his little sister's frivolity, which he regarded as unworthy of the family's position. According to Pocahontas's later revelations to Prince Charles, who subsequently became Charles I, the elder of her brothers summoned her to his house, the second-largest dwelling in Powhatan's compound, and delivered long addresses to her, urging her to become more aware of her position.

But a girl of nine or ten who was high-spirited and intelligent and who had too little to keep her occupied could not be long suppressed. She is believed to have been about ten when the most notorious incident of her childhood took place.

The sequence of events began innocently when she went off on a hunting trip with Piaoko and two of his friends, all of them junior warriors. The Chickahominy system of chaperonage was informal, the girl had not yet reached the age of puberty and the presence of her brother was sufficient to satisfy the tribe's conventions. The quartet traveled southward, and presumably Pocahontas's aunts knew her general whereabouts.

By the sheerest of coincidences a party of eight or ten Tuscarora braves arrived at the Chickahominy town a day or two later, during the absence of Powhatan's two younger children. The group was led by a nephew of the Tuscarora's Great Sachem, a man whose position in his own confederation was similar to that of the Chickahominy Chief of Chiefs.

Relations between these two nations were always delicate, so Powhatan took special care to order that a feast be held in honor of his equal's nephew. Whole sides of venison were roasted, slabs of bear bacon were removed from the storage bins and hunters went out to snare wildfowl for the event. The sisters of the Chief of Chiefs must have been in charge of the food preparations, and small children were sent out into the forest to gather some of the rare fruits that were served only on such occasions.

Apparently Powhatan had been either preoccupied or indifferent, because it was only during this period prior to the feast that he became aware of the absence of Piaoko and Pocahontas. He was not worried about the boy because a junior warrior was expected to take care of himself in any situation, and if he failed, he was expected to suffer the consequences. But the fact that Pocahontas was not present was an altogether different matter, and Powhatan became alarmed.

How he conceived the false idea that his daughter—and, presumably, his younger son—had fallen into the hands of the Tuscarora and had been killed is one of those tantalizing mysteries for which no solution has ever been found. The mere presence of the relatively large band of his people's traditional enemies in the domain of the Chickahominy may have been responsible. In any event, and for whatever his reasons, the Chief of Chiefs convinced himself that Pocahontas had met a violent end at the hands of the Tuscarora.

The laws of Indian hospitality forbade the murder of the visitors while they were guests in the main town of the Chickahominy, so Powhatan arranged that they be taken on a hunting trip prior to the feast and slain in the wilderness. The supposed death of Pocahontas could be avenged only by a member of the royal family, and Mataoko begged for the honor, a wish his father granted. The whole matter had the gravest of implications, as the killing of the Tuscarora Great Sachem's nephew by the elder son of the Chickahominy Chief of Chiefs would make it inevitable that the two most powerful confederations of tribes in what would become the American South soon would be at war.

Careful arrangements were made for the day-long hunting trip, and the unsuspecting Tuscarora went out into the forests with a party of their hosts, Mataoko remaining close beside the man he intended to kill. Before the deed could be accomplished, however, the hunters heard approaching human sounds. Mataoko was dumbfounded when he was confronted by his carefree brother and sister, happily returning home from their own expedition, which had lasted several days longer than they had intended.

Mataoko quickly cancelled the murder plans, went through the motions of the day's hunt, and thereafter the feast in honor of the Tuscarora was held as scheduled. Piaoko and Pocahontas were present at this occasion, the youth taking a place in the circle of adult males at the meal, while Pocahontas joined her aunts and other high-born women and served the men. The storm did not break until the Tuscarora departed for their own home, escorted to the ill-defined wilderness border of the two nations by a large party of Chickahominy warriors. The visitors never learned how close they had come to losing their lives, or by what a narrow margin a major war had been averted.

Piaoko's punishment was relatively mild: he was sent off into the wilderness for ten days and nights, armed only with a knife, and was required to survive by his own efforts. This was not a difficult feat for one who had already become a junior brave and consequently knew most of the forest's secrets.

But Pocahontas's personal situation was drastically changed. Thereafter she is known to have been much closer to her father, silently attending him at Council meetings and on the infrequent occasions when he adjudicated major disputes between his subjects. Of far greater importance in the girl's daily life, she was taken from the jurisdiction of her aunts, who obviously could no longer handle her, and was placed under the direct supervision of the stern and unyielding Mataoko.

The heir to the throne of the Chickahominy was married at about that same time to the first of his wives, a girl still in her teens who belonged to the clan of the Bi-tan, the only family of sufficiently high birth to become the squaw of the future head of the Chickahominy Confederation. Nothing else is known about the bride other than that she lived only for a year or two after the marriage. There is no information available to indicate the nature of her relations with her young sister-in-law, in whose company she must have spent much of her time.

Pocahontas undoubtedly continued to dwell in the same hut she had occupied in Powhatan's compound since she had passed her seventh summer. But now her chores were assigned by Mataoko, to whom she had to report her daily accomplishments. He was wise to the ways of children, knew her tricks and tolerated none of them. In addition to working longer hours in the fields, devoting more time to cooking and attending her other chores with greater devotion, Pocahontas had to listen to long daily lectures on such subjects as duty, honor and the history of the family of Powhatan. Many years later, when sympathizing with Charles Stuart, whose duties and responsibilities multiplied after the death of his elder brother, Henry, made him Prince of Wales, Pocahontas told the heir to the throne of England and Scotland that she knew how heavy his burden must be. She also revealed her sense of humor when she said it was "unfortunate" that Mataoko was the greatest orator in a family long renowned for its speechmakers, and that he had obtained much of his practice in the art at her expense.

In the long run, not even a man as strong and intelligent as Mataoko was a match for the charm and feminine cunning of Pocahontas. Few details are available regarding their growing rapport over the next few years, but one fact is of major significance and speaks for itself. On one of Mataoko's first visits to Jamestown his magnificent, multicolored feather cloak was much admired by the settlers, to whom he proudly revealed that it had been made for him by his beloved sister. Obviously Pocahontas had her stern brother and supervisor twisted around her seemingly delicate little finger, and it wasn't long before she once again was doing as she pleased.

VI

The most important of permanent changes took place
in the life of Pocahontas when she reached puberty,
presumably around the age of thirteen. At approximately this
same time, although the girl did not yet know it, a small band
of hardy and courageous Englishmen landed on the coast of
what they called Virginia and established the settlement of
Jamestown at the mouth of the James River, a march of about
two to three days through the forests for a skilled
Chickahominy warrior. As these foreigners recorded time, the
year was 1607.

   With the arrival of her physical womanhood

Pocahontas had to abandon her merry ways and adopt a more sober and circumspect approach to life. She had no choice because the consequences of disobedience now could be disastrous, even for the daughter of the Chief of Chiefs. The supervision of a girl's life from her thirteenth summer to her sixteenth was all-encompassing, and all taboos had to be strictly observed. Any departure from tradition would be severely punished, and there were no exceptions to the rules.

If a girl lost her virginity, or if she spent time alone with any male other than a close blood relative under circumstances that might lead the elderly women of the community to believe she had lost her virginity, she would become a social pariah and would be compelled to spend the rest of her life as a prostitute. Her eyebrows would be plucked, her hair would be cut shorter than shoulder length and, in addition to working without respite in the fields all day, she would be required to live in special quarters, which men of the town and guests could visit at will after sundown. Not even a girl's standing as the daughter of the Chief of Chiefs could protect her if it was believed or even suspected that she had lost her virginity. What she did after her sixteenth summer was her own concern; she was free then to enjoy relations with a man without fear of stigma or punishment, but until that time her person was taboo.

For three years she would be permitted to eat no fish or shellfish, nor could she drink the broth in which seafood had been cooked. Her special status was marked by a red flower, which she was required to wear in her hair at all times, and by a band of red-dyed shells at the hem of her loose-fitting dress, which she now wore calf-length. She was forbidden to braid her hair now, and it cascaded freely down her back, as it had done in her earliest childhood. She would continue to wear it in this style until she married, at which time she would fix it permanently in a halo braid.

Girls in the special thirteen- to sixteen-year-old group were not allowed to swim at times when others in the town went down to the river. Instead they swam at an appointed time of their own, and were attended by tough-minded old squaws armed with clubs. Any young brave who had the temerity to wander down to the river at that hour risked a severe beating, and any maiden who dared to speak to him or acknowledge his proximity was thrashed, too.

Pocahontas and the other girls of her age group were moved into a long house of their own, and no man, not even the Chief of Chiefs, was allowed to set foot inside the place. The girls and the old squaws who chaperoned and supervised them ate all of their meals at a cooking pit behind the long house, out of sight of the rest of the town. Only at special times and for special feasts was a girl permitted to visit the compound of her family. Even on these occasions she was escorted by one of the old women.

The isolation of the group from the rest of the community was complete in every way. When the warriors competed at games of skill and endurance, a frequent event in the spring, summer and autumn that attracted visitors from other villages and from satellite tribes, the girls of thirteen to sixteen summers attended in a body, their chaperones much in evidence, and sat apart from everyone else. No man approached that area, and a warrior who kicked or threw a ball near the group incurred the wrath of the old squaws, which even the most courageous brave was wise to avoid.

If it was deemed necessary or desirable, Pocahontas could be visited by her father or Mataoko, who were admitted inside the palisade of sharpened logs that surrounded the maidens' long house. Piaoko was a bachelor, so he was not permitted to enter the compound under any circumstances, even though he was a member of the royal family. This was a wise precaution: the Chickahominy did not fear incest, which they regarded as abominable, but it might have been possible for the clever Piaoko to arrange a rendezvous with one of Pocahontas's friends while ostensibly visiting his sister.

Numbers of senior warriors stood sentry duty outside the palisade when groups of visitors came to the town of the Chickahominy, permitting no one to approach the area and keeping the adolescent girls inside. And although there had been no war in Pocahontas's lifetime, she undoubtedly learned that a permanent guard was established around the palisade when there were hostilities with other nations.

The total, strictly enforced isolation of the maidens is significant when it is remembered that Jamestown was settled around the very time that Pocahontas entered the long house of the unmarried girls. On her first visit to Jamestown several years later, in the company of her father and both of her brothers, she revealed that she had been almost overcome with curiosity about the strangers because, due to her isolation, she had not seen any of the Englishmen who had come to the town of the Chickahominy to trade weapons, mirrors, blankets and iron cooking utensils for food and furs. She was one of the few inhabitants of the town, therefore, who never caught even a glimpse of the visitors.

This is most significant in relation to the myth about the alleged romance of Pocahontas and Captain John Smith, which, had it taken place, would have occurred during her period of isolation, prior to her first visit to Jamestown. The story and its origins will be discussed in detail in subsequent chapters. It is sufficient at this time to note that because of Pocahontas's presence in the long house of the maidens at the time Smith was supposedly captured by Chickahominy warriors, brought to the town and placed under sentence of death by Powhatan, only to be reprieved because Pocahontas begged that he be spared, the story could not have been true, by the girl's own admission.

One thing is certain: life in the long house of the maidens was tantamount to a three-year jail sentence. There were those who escaped, to be sure, but a girl who was discovered was ruined for the rest of her life.

The supervision of the maidens was so strict and their isolation so complete that they were not even permitted to work in the fields outside the town, which must have pleased Pocahontas. The girls had a small corn patch and a vegetable garden of their own inside their palisade, but their crops required little tending in such a confined area, and could not have kept them busy for more than a short time each day. Presumably the crops were grown there so the maidens would not forget what they had learned earlier in their childhood.

In the main the girls had very little to occupy their time. They made clothes, learned to primp a bit, kept their quarters clean. They heard lectures on subjects long familiar to them, and presumably they were taught legends and songs they did not already know. Most of their time was spent gossiping, and it is fairly safe to guess that, like adolescent girls throughout all history, the principal subject of their conversation was boys. Clay was packed into the chinks between the logs of their palisades, however, so they could not even catch a glimpse of the young Chickahominy braves during the years of their incarceration, and it must have been frustrating for them to realize that these were the same youths with whom they had associated so freely earlier in their lives.

It was this realization, drilled in over three dreary years, that was the key to the practice of locking away the maidens. The Chickahominy were one of the most industrious of the Indian nations, and at first glance it appears strange that they would have permitted groups of their healthiest young women to spend three years in unproductive idleness. What they were doing, however, was impressing on the maidens their new status as women, and as nearly as can be judged from a distance of more than three and a half centuries, the system was effective. The girls who were locked in the long house of the maidens had ample opportunity to think about their future, and most were eager to take their places as active members of society when they were released at the end of the sixteenth summer.

Certainly it was not coincidental that the maidens were highly prized by the community, and that most girls were married soon after they left the isolation of the long house. A jealous warrior could be sure that the young squaw he married had slept with no other man, and the girl, hungry for sex as well as the companionship of a husband, was eager to be married. So everyone benefited, even though it can well be argued that a girl acquired the new habit of laziness during the years she spent apart from the mainstream of Chickahominy life. On the other hand, the pressures of the society were great, and the need to grow crops, prepare meals and make clothes forced a girl to resume the active life she had led before her thirteenth summer.

At some time fairly early in Pocahontas's stay at the long house of the maidens, probably in 1609, her father presented her with a mirror that had been a gift of the strangers from the far side of the Great Sea. A small square of highly burnished metal, the mirror had a deep and long-lasting

53

effect on Pocahontas. For the first time in her life she was able to study her reflection in detail and to confirm what others had long known, that she was far more attractive than other Chickahominy girls. At no time had she felt a sense of inferiority in any way, nor should she have suffered even twinges of such feelings, but now her femininity was bolstered. This inner sense of security would be of the greatest importance to her in the unique life that lay ahead, when she would part with the past of her own people and enjoy experiences that no other Indian had ever known.

As a symbol, and as much more than that, the mirror became her most cherished possession. Eventually she would own others, larger and more ornate, but her first mirror was a treasure she kept until the end of her life. Thereafter it was a family heirloom, and although battered and scratched, it was handed down from one generation to the next by her descendants until, around the time of the American War of Independence, it vanished, never to reappear.

The mirror was the first product of a civilization other than her own that Pocahontas ever saw, and it excited her imagination. Until she received it she had probably never dreamed that there might be a world beyond that of the Chickahominy Confederation and the realms of its neighbors, where life was similar to that which she knew. Now the realization that there were men whose ways differed from those of the Indians in every respect must have shattered the equanimity of a girl whose quick intelligence enabled her to grasp far-reaching implications. Although she could not have guessed the roles she was destined to play, it is not surprising that she soon became dissatisfied with her own lot and longed for a part on a larger and better-developed stage.

Even the most optimistic of teen-aged girls in Pocahontas's situation must have known that her prospects in the land of her own people were drab. And as far back as she could remember, Pocahontas had understood that her position was unlike that of her contemporaries. This knowledge was reinforced during her stay in the long house of the maidens.

Her friends could look forward to early marriages to young, vigorous braves after their "graduation" from the long house, but no such future awaited the daughter of Powhatan. Her high birth excluded her from marriage to anyone other than warriors of the clan of the Bi-tan, and there were no eligible bachelors in that family who were suitable for her. Lady de la Warr, subsequently explaining and perhaps rationalizing the marriage of the Indian princess to John Rolfe, went into some detail on the matter.

The Bi-tan had two small nephews or grandnephews, but both were eight or ten years younger than Pocahontas. It would be embarrassing, even degrading, for her to be forced to wait until they grew to manhood before she married, and by that time neither of the young braves would want to take a squaw who was so much older. The only alternative was equally unpleasant. The sons and nephews of the Bi-tan already had wives, but the mortality rate among Chickahominy women was high, so it was possible that one of them would become a widower within a reasonable period after Pocahontas's release from the long house. In that event a suitor eligible for her hand could make the necessary arrangements with Powhatan.

Had she been of lesser birth she could have become a junior wife of some warrior in the Bi-tan's family, where polygamy was practiced. But it was unthinkable that the highest-ranking girl in the nation, who stood ahead of all other females, including Mataoko's squaw, should become the second or third wife of one of the Bi-tan's relatives, hold an inferior position and take orders from the first wife, a woman of necessarily lower birth. Therefore she would have to wait until one of them became a widower.

Until the coming of the English settlers to Jamestown no genuine alternative had offered itself to Pocahontas, and even when she learned of the presence of the strangers on the shores of what had long been considered the land of the Chickahominy, it is improbable that she thought to escape from her delicate and frustrating situation. That prospect must have grown in her mind only after she had visited Jamestown and had become acquainted with some of the settlers.

It must be stressed that Pocahontas had not been dissatisfied with her existence. While it is true that she was unusually high-spirited and had engaged in far more escapades than most members of her sex, she had never rebelled against the authority of her father or that of either the Bi-tan or Mataoko. Fundamentally she had violated none of the taboos of the Chickahominy, and throughout her adolescence, up to the time of her release from the long house of the maidens in her sixteenth summer, she dutifully accepted her fate and followed the routines that were expected of her.

She endured her incarceration with the resignation for which the Chickahominy were noted, emerging from her ordeal with her high spirits unbroken and her zest for life unimpaired. She was regarded as a woman now, and neither Mataoko nor her aunts had any right to exercise authority over her. In fact, she was required to obey only one person, her father.

Upon leaving the long house of the maidens, Pocahontas moved back into her own hut in the compound of her father. Now, within the limits prescribed by Chickahominy law and tradition, she could do as she pleased. It was her privilege to swim with others, to go on hunting and fishing trips with Piaoko and his friends, and—for the first time—to visit her own friends and receive visits from them. Her only responsibility was that of working for a portion of each day in the fields, weather permitting, but the passage of time had made her no more eager to do such work, so she discharged her obligation by doing the minimum required of her.

It is not known whether Pocahontas engaged in affairs with any of the warriors of the tribe during this period of her life. But, as the most attractive girl in the town, she undoubtedly would have excited male interest, and a warrior whose lower birth prevented him from marrying her was nevertheless free to pay court to her and, with her consent, to make love to her.

The question arises because of her later situation in Jamestown, where she showed no interest in the bachelors of the community and they, in turn, did not become her suitors. Young Englishmen who expected to return to their own homes were required by their own taboos to marry virgins.

And the man Pocahontas did marry was a widower, and therefore may have been more relaxed in his sexual standards.

Pocahontas and her husband maintained a discreet silence on the subject, and none of their contemporaries speculated on the matter in their letters or indicated that they possessed any positive knowledge. So it is unlikely that the question will ever by answered definitively.

Of far greater importance, although Pocahontas herself could not have realized it at the time, there occurred an incident that was innocent and seemingly trivial. Out of it, however, grew the legend of the romance of the Chickahominy princess and Captain John Smith.

One day in the winter of 1610 a party of Chickahominy braves who were hunting not far from the town came across a young boy from Jamestown. The child, one of the youngest of the settlers, was no more than twelve years of age. Hungry, tired and badly frightened, he had wandered away from the English settlement, and seeking food, had gone exploring in the wilderness. Knowing nothing about forests, he had lost his way, and for the better part of a week had been stumbling through the underbrush, trying to make his way back to the English outpost at the mouth of the James River.

The warriors brought him to the town of the Chickahominy, where his presence excited little general interest. It must be remembered that most residents of the community had grown accustomed to seeing their neighbors. But Pocahontas had never set eyes on one of these strangers; now, suddenly, she had an opportunity to study one at length.

She gave the boy a meal she prepared for him herself, and he ate ravenously. She saw to it that he received lodging in the long house of the boys, and for a number of days she spent the better part of her own time with the lad, communicating with him as best she could in sign language.

He was treated with great kindness throughout his stay, and soon recovered his health. When he was strong enough to travel, Pocahontas made arrangements for an escort, and a senior warrior guided the boy back to his own people. If Pocahontas heard his name during his brief sojourn with the

Chickahominy, she could not pronounce it. He, however, knew her name and rank, and when he returned to Jamestown, he sang the praises of the lovely Indian princess who had treated him so generously.

As far as Pocahontas was concerned, the incident whetted her curiosity about the strange breed who had crossed the Great Sea and were making their home in her father's domain. The event had no other significance to her.

After the boy told his story, it was duly recorded in official correspondence with London and in private letters. As will be seen, John Smith, who was absent from Jamestown at the time, was told of the incident on his return and did not forget it. And years later, under circumstances that neither he nor anyone else could have forseen, he used it for his own purposes, unknowingly creating a legend that has never died.

VII

In order to understand the next phase in the life of Pocahontas and all that happened thereafter, it is necessary to go back a few years and examine the origin and beginnings of the Jamestown colony. The story really begins during the brilliant reign of Queen Elizabeth I in England, when such great sea captains as Sir Francis Drake and Sir John Hawkins created a fever of sustained excitement over the discovery and exploration of New World lands across the Atlantic Ocean.

One of the greatest of the explorers was the complete Renaissance man, Sir Walter Raleigh, a soldier and statesman, a sailor and courtier and author. Although he never visited

North America himself, he expended enormous energy and spent vast sums of money in an attempt to establish a permanent colony, in 1584, on or near Roanoke Island in what is now North Carolina. He named the land in honor of his patroness, Elizabeth, the "Virgin Queen." The colony met a succession of disasters and the effort failed, but Virginia remained prominent in the minds of men who wanted to establish an empire in the New World and, more important in their minds, to bring back ships laden with gold and precious gems, as the Spaniards long had been doing in Central and South America.

Raleigh fell from favor when Elizabeth was succeeded, in 1603, by James VI of Scotland, who became James I of England, and was confined in the Tower of London on suspicion of treason. There he remained for thirteen years, writing his *History of the World*, fighting in vain to clear his name and obtain his freedom. In spite of his unjust incarceration he continued to exert great influence in aristocratic and commercial circles.

King James, the son of Mary, Queen of Scots, who had been beheaded by Elizabeth, was one of the most complex men of his own or any other age. A mercurial, temperamental Scotsman, he was dour but given to flights of euphoria. His personal tastes were bisexual. He regarded himself as an intellectual, surrounded himself with scholars and commissioned the preparation of the new translation of the Bible that has borne his name. He also distinguished himself by writing the first treatise in history condemning the use of tobacco. Suspicious, vacillating and arrogant, he was endowed with all of the characteristics that made members of the house of Stuart the most inconsistent rulers in the history of Great Britain.

In addition to everything else, James was an eccentric, and one of the most pronounced of his traits was his parsimony, caused at least in part by the financial deprivations he had suffered before being called to the throne of England. Like many of his prominent subjects, he envied the bulging royal treasure houses of Spain. It was true, to be sure, that Drake, Hawkins and other English pirates, calling themselves by the more polite name of privateers, had robbed

Spanish galleons on the high seas, making England wealthy in the process. The Crown received fifty percent of the loot, but James was greedy, and agreed with those of his subjects who believed that England's wealth—and their own—would multiply far more rapidly if Englishmen found their own gold, silver, diamond, ruby and emerald mines in the New World.

A number of attempts were made by Raleigh and others to establish New World colonies during the reign of Elizabeth, but these efforts dwindled in her late years, when other matters occupied her mind and she lost interest in the subject. But the great nobles and wealthy merchants renewed their interest when James came to the throne. They discussed the subject with him and he encouraged them, but his terms caused many to back away. He demanded fifty percent of the profits but refused to put up a farthing of royal funds to organize an expedition, and some of his subjects thought his price was too high.

Several dreamers persisted, however, and late in 1605 a commercial organization calling itself the London Company was formed. King James graciously granted these good gentlemen a charter—on his own terms—that gave them the right to set up a colony in his New World domain of Virginia and to extract its wealth for their mutual benefit. Armed with this document, the promoters of the scheme made the rounds of aristocrats and other men of wealth, raising funds. They also went to Sir Walter Raleigh, who was languishing in the Tower, and he freely gave them the benefit of his advice, telling them in detail how to avoid the errors and pitfalls that he and his colleagues had suffered more than two decades earlier. The London Company encountered many difficulties of its own, but in time the money was raised and recruits were gathered for the expedition.

The sponsors of the enterprise included some of the most powerful men in the realm. Chief among them was King James's elder son, Henry, Prince of Wales, the heir to the throne, who was more far-seeing than most of his contemporaries and, unlike his father, was interested primarily in discovery and colonization for their own sakes. He, in turn, was influenced by Archdeacon Richard Hakluyt, the great geographer who inspired, directed and advised those who conducted virtually every English voyage of exploration in the late sixteenth and early seventeenth centuries. Sir John Popham, the Lord Chief Justice, was a major investor, and so was Ludovic Stuart, Duke of Richmond and the King's kinsman.

The men they hired to lead the expedition were the most competent gentlemen-adventurers to be found anywhere, and many were so enthusiastic they invested their own funds in the Company. Three ships were purchased, the largest of them a relatively new vessel, the one hundred-ton, square-rigged *Susan Constant*, which was large enough, by seventeenth-century standards, to carry two cannon, large quantities of supplies and seventy passengers. She would serve as the flagship of the little fleet's commodore, Captain Christopher Newport, a blunt, aggressive man who had spent the better part of his life at sea and was rightly regarded by his superiors as reliable and worthy of their highest trust.

The second-in-command was the lean, introverted Captain Bartholomew Gosnold, who not only had sailed with Newport on numerous occasions but had a distinguished record of his own, having conducted a successful voyage of discovery to the New World in 1602. His ship, the *God Speed*, which had a gross displacement of forty tons, was an old vessel, but both Gosnold and Newport said she was seaworthy, and the directors of the London Company accepted their judgment.

The third master, Captain John Ratcliffe, was recommended by his colleagues, who knew him slightly. They had no idea he was a moody man hampered by a sadistic streak and a temper he could not control. His ship, the *Discovery*, was a tiny, twenty-ton pinnace, and Ratcliffe proved he was a seaman, if nothing more, by sailing the ship across the Atlantic.

The man on whom the directors placed the greatest reliance was Edward Maria Wingfield, a man of financial substance whose patrician airs made a deep impression on his superiors. He was austere, high-minded and dedicated, but he was one of those men whom nature destined to be a bumbler. Mentally slow and physically awkward, he was narrow-minded, almost always formed the wrong conclusions and proved to be more of a liability than an asset.

Master George Percy, the younger brother of a Company director, the Earl of Northumberland, was a once-wealthy playboy who had dissipated his inheritance and may have been induced to join the expedition because his presence in England was an embarrassment to his family. A bearer of one of England's oldest names, Percy was an amiable young man, too easily influenced, but he was courageous and came to believe in the worth of the venture.

Captain John Martin, about whom little is known, had been an artillery officer in the army. He was honest and conscientious, but his health was frail and prevented him from contributing more than he did to his colleagues.

Captain George Kendal, who was acquainted only with Ratcliffe at the beginning of the long journey, was a former infantry officer, a vindictive mischief-maker who was responsible for the near-collapse of the expedition and eventually was executed on ill-defined charges of treason.

The Reverend Robert Hunt was the expedition's chaplain. Pious, self-effacing and calm, he refused to take part in the incessant quarrels that marred the relations of the other gentlemen. In times of crisis this quiet giant demonstrated his physical and moral courage, and proved his worth on scores of occasions.

Captain Gabriel Archer was the youngest son of a baronet who had served briefly in a Household regiment, then had fought as a mercenary in the Netherlands. He was quick-witted, flamboyant and ambitious, at all times a man of action rather than a thinker, and his virtues were outweighed by his rashness.

In all, the expedition numbered one hundred and fifty men, among them carpenters, bricklayers, dockhands and stonemasons. There were two surgeon-barbers, a few former sailors, a one-time drummer in a military band and several boys, two or three of them not yet in their teens.

The least-known member of the band of gentlemen at the time the expedition left England, an oversight he himself subsequently corrected, was one John Smith, a self-styled

Captain, the son of a prosperous Lincolnshire gentleman farmer, who had been born on January 2, 1579. One of the true geniuses of his era, Smith discovered portions of Virginia and Chesapeake Bay, New England and its Cape Cod, both of which he named. At the time he joined the expedition he had served as a mercenary in a number of foreign armies, had seen service in many parts of Europe, and had traveled extensively in the Near Eastern domains of the Ottoman Empire, in Russia and in the interior of Africa.

He was an author of great talent who wrote eight books about his many journeys and voyages, all of them successful, and his works on North America were directly responsible for the migration of thousands from the British Isles to the New World. Translations of his works also were influential in the mass movement of whole families to America from France, Holland and the German principalities.

Although he totally lacked training as a cartographer, Smith's North American maps were marvelously accurate, and have been used as models of the cartographer's art down to the present day. They were also influential as aids to his good friend, Henry Hudson, who used them on his own voyages of discovery. Like Raleigh, Smith was a blazing success in everything he did: he was a brilliant soldier, sailor and navigator; his books were considered authoritative for a century and a half after his own time; and his portraits were as effective as his maps. The great propagandist in the colonization of North America, he, more than any other man, introduced the New World to the Old.

Smith also had his weaknesses. He spent money recklessly, and although he lived on a handsome scale, he died penniless. His zest for life and his ambition were boundless; a lifelong bachelor, he had many love affairs, some with the wives of his patrons and friends. Perhaps his greatest fault was his inability to see or write about himself with the honesty he displayed in his evaluations of others. He was so anxious to create a good impression that he could not resist embellishing his own exploits. At times he merely exaggerated, but when it suited his purposes, he did not hesitate to lie—magnificently.

There were strange quirks in his nature. He never proved he had held an officer's rank in any army, yet he always called himself Captain. He legitimately held the title of President of Virginia, a post to which he was elected. He held a warrant, signed by King James, naming him Grand Admiral of New England and the Fishing Banks. And his friends in the New World, grateful for his efforts in preventing the collapse of their colony in its time of greatest peril, hailed him as the Savior of Jamestown. Yet he referred to himself exclusively as Captain John Smith until his death at the age of fifty-two.

Virtually all of the ladies in his life were blondes, but he is remembered neither for these exuberant romances nor for his many legitimate exploits. His name lives only because of a myth—perpetrated by Smith himself for reasons he regarded as valid at the time.

The settlement of the Pilgrims in New England was the direct outgrowth of Smith's explorations several years earlier, and few people in modern times realize he was hired as military leader of that expedition. When he failed, at the last moment, to appear for that voyage, Captain Miles Standish was hired in his stead and sailed on the *Mayflower*.

No one was more aware of the paradoxes in his life than Smith himself. A few years before his death he is said to have remarked, "I did not take up the habit of smoking a pipe until long after I had sold, at a loss, the acres on whose soil grows the finest tobacco to be found in this world."

Smith's greatest years lay directly ahead when, in 1606, he and his colleagues began to prepare for the voyage to Virginia. Supplies included rice and oatmeal, rather than the wheat and rye that spoiled more quickly. The stores also included sugar, prunes, raisins and spices that made most dishes tolerable. Beef was pickled, pork and fish were salted, and there were quantities of mutton in butter-lined pots. Beer and cider were provided for everyone, and the gentlemen also drank claret, Canary and Madeira. At Newport's insistence there was no brandywine or gin, as the gentry were inclined to quarrel when they consumed hard spirits.

On January 1, 1607, the company of one hundred and fifty-two persons sailed from London on board the three ships after attending a special service at Westminster Abbey. The weather was so foul that Commodore Newport was forced to anchor for twenty-four hours before he could leave the

Thames River and sail into the English Channel, so the beginning of the momentous journey was inauspicious.

In mid-February the ships reached the Canary Islands, and paused long enough to take on fresh stores of water and additional supplies of meat before making their run across the Atlantic. The weather was surprisingly pleasant, but the voyage was boring, and Smith quarreled with Archer and Kendal. They insisted he had drawn his sword without provocation, and summoned the other gentlemen to a "trial," which they held in the main saloon of the *Susan Constant*. Newport and his officers refused to attend, and when Smith was "condemned to death by hanging" when land was reached, he laughed in the faces of the men who had become his enemies.

On March 24 the three vessels reached the island of Hispanola in the Caribbean, which had been discovered by Columbus. The entire company went ashore, but instead of enjoying the land and the fresh food available, some of the gentlemen built a gallows. They made only one miscalculation: in order to hang Smith they had to take him into custody. But he was a superb swordsman and an equally able pistol shot, and his foes, eight in number, were not his match. Commodore Newport, assisted by Martin and the Reverend Mr. Hunt, dissuaded the foolish gentlemen from trying to carry out their scheme.

Smith was scornful, and indicated his feelings in *True Relation*, his book on the Jamestown colony's early days. "I had oft faced far greater odds," he declared, "and knew there was no swordsman in that miserable lot who could stand up to me with impunity."

The crisis eased, and for the next two and a half weeks the company moved from one Caribbean island to another, eating fresh food, exploring and thoroughly enjoying life. On April 10 they sailed due north, but a gale blew them far out into the Atlantic, and some of the gentlemen agreed with Captain Ratcliffe that the expedition should return to England. But Commodore Newport, strongly supported by Captain John Smith, insisted they go on to their original destination, and his will prevailed.

One day in early April another gale struck the ships, but this time they were blown into what became known as the Gulf Stream, and on April 26 they sighted land. The crude charts they had obtained from Admiral Sir Walter Raleigh convinced Newport they had reached their destination, and the more devout members of the company agreed with the Reverend Mr. Hunt that Divine Providence had guided them.

Shortly before nightfall they edged cautiously into the waters that Captain John Smith would name Chesapeake Bay, and anchored until morning. The gentlemen and officers of all three ships gathered in the main saloon of the *Susan Constant*, and the sealed orders of the directors of the London Company were opened. The adventurers received a number of specific instructions: 1) to aid in the construction and maintenance of a strong merchant fleet, which would become a part of the Royal Navy in time of war; 2) to train "able mariners" for the protection of England and Scotland; 3) to "spread the Gospel among the heathen people of Virginia"; 4) to plant and develop an English Protestant colony in a part of the world that was coming increasingly under the influence and domination of Catholic Spain; 5) to "establish new areas for English trade"; 6) to devote their foremost efforts to "the finding of gold, silver and other precious metals, and also to the finding of gold, emeralds, sapphires, ruby stones and other brilliants."

In order to carry out these directives the men were told to form a Council of State, which would hold office for one year. Its membership was to include the three ships' captains, Newport, Gosnold and Ratcliffe, and four of the gentleman-adventurers, Edward Wingfield, John Martin, George Kendal and Captain John Smith. Enmity to Smith flared again, and his foes voted to deny him his seat. He could have insisted on his rights, but conferred privately with Newport, and together they decided that, for the present, the preservation of unity was the paramount consideration. At the appropriate time Smith would claim his seat.

On the morning of May 13, 1607, watched by unseen figures lurking in the forests of dark green that swept down to the banks, the ships' boats were lowered and the adventurers went ashore. Commodore Newport raised the Union Jack, Captain Smith planted the personal banner of Prince Henry, and the colony of Jamestown came into being.

VIII

Behind the fringe of pines that formed a natural waterfront barrier stood a pleasant meadow, bounded on one side by what appeared to be a large river and on the other by a brook with exceptionally sweet water. The members of the expedition decided to make their colony there, and work was started without delay on two projects, the building of wooden huts that would enable the men to move ashore from the ships, and the construction of a shallop, with a mainmast and foremast, that could carry approximately twenty-five men and would be used for the exploration of inland waters.

The entire company enjoyed good health, and in the

first days there were only two casualties, one of them minor. Gabriel Archer, trying to set an example, wielded an ax with such vigor that he severely blistered the palms of his hands and had to rest. Matthew Morton, a sailor, joined one of the tree-chopping parties, and being unfamiliar with the handling of an ax, almost severed a leg.

The Englishmen did not know it, but they were under constant surveillance. Their ships had been seen from a distance on the day they had sailed into Chesapeake Bay, and thereafter scouts from the nearest fishing village of the Chickahominy, about ten miles distant, had sent an unending stream of reports to their chief, who had relayed the word to Powhatan.

The Chief of Chiefs, ever cautious, wanted to determine the intention of the strangers before driving them from his realm. They were small in number, so he did not doubt his ability to destroy them, but they appeared to be a very odd breed, and he had no desire to suffer needless casualties. These men with white skins and hairy faces wore breastplates of shining metal and carried remarkably long knives. They were also equipped with fire sticks, but Powhatan and his Council were not afraid of these weapons, having learned that members of the landing party had made a number of attempts to bring down ducks and geese, but had failed. As any wilderness dweller knew, wildfowl could not be shot, but had to be snared when they landed on ponds and rivers.

Powhatan was curious, too, about a number of tools and other implements the strange men carried. They lighted their fires with an instrument that made sparks, which the Indians would discover was called a tinderbox and flint, and a tool called a saw was effective in cutting even the biggest oak, elm and maple trees into long, smooth slabs of wood.

But it was obvious the strangers knew nothing about the wilderness. They searched the forest for food, rejoicing when they found berries and nuts, but they trampled on some of the most delicious edible plants and ignored others. Sometimes they went hunting, too, but made so much noise as they crashed through the underbrush that they frightened away the animals they were seeking. When one of the company suffered from an upset stomach and went off into the forest to retch, help was within reach, but he didn't know it. He could have picked and chewed the leaves of a small, aromatic herb that would have cured his condition instantly.

The strangers used axes of heavy metal that were marvelously sharp, but they wielded the tools so ineptly that the Chickahominy scouts found it difficult not to laugh aloud. The ignorant foreigners spent hours trying to burn logs of a young elm, and they were building some of their houses so close to the banks of what would be called the James River that the buildings would be swept away when the waters rose in the autumn and spring. Worst of all, the town was being constructed in the spongy meadowland, where the climate was so damp that anyone who stayed there for any length of time eventually sickened and died.

The strategy adopted by Powhatan was simple but cunning. He would not allow his subjects to reveal their presence until the strangers grew weaker and their need for food required them to behave meekly. Then, if they became aggressive instead, it would be an easy matter to send hundreds of warriors against them and push them into the sea.

Whether Pocahontas learned of the landing of the Englishmen in the first weeks of Jamestown's existence is not known. As nearly as can be ascertained, she entered the long house of the maidens at about the time the original landing was made, so even if she and the other girls heard the news from the old squaws who supervised them, she was too isolated to ask questions or find out more than the bare essentials. Many weeks would pass before the Chickahominy discovered and analyzed enough information about the customs and practices of the intruders to pass judgment on them. In the meantime the people of the Chickahominy, Pocahontas included, were compelled to wait until the Chief of Chiefs changed his tactics.

Meanwhile the neophyte colonists, still not realizing that every move they made was under observation, blithely continued to establish their colony, their optimism far greater than the reality of their situation warranted. Wingfield supervised the men working on the houses, Newport was in charge of building the shallop, and the restless Smith led a party inland on a trip of exploration that followed the river. After marching about eight miles they found a recently abandoned campfire, the first evidence of a native civilization they had seen. They had no way of knowing that the warriors, following Powhatan's orders, had vanished rather than be forced into a confrontation with the strangers.

Scattered around the fire were empty oyster shells, and the Englishmen were elated when they found a vine basket filled with unopened oysters. They roasted them immediately, and Smith later wrote they were "very delicate." Nearby they also discovered wild strawberry vines, and even though the season was early, they picked a large number of enormous, ripe berries.

Soon thereafter Newport went for a brief sail in the shallop, returning with a vast quantity of oysters and mussels. Smith drew his first maps of the area, calling the point of land adjoining the mouth of the river Point Comfort, to the east of which lay the open Atlantic and to the north Chesapeake Bay. The peninsula that jutted out at the southern end of the Bay was named Cape Henry, in honor of the Prince of Wales, and a peninsula to the north was called Cape Charles, after the Prince's younger brother, then the Duke of York.

No one appreciated the New World vistas more than John Smith, who wrote: "Here is a country that may have the prerogative over the most pleasant places of Europe, Asia, Africa, or America, for large and pleasant navigable rivers; heaven and earth never agreed better to frame a place for man's habitation being of our constitutions, were it fully manured and inhabited by industrious people. Here are mountains, hills, plains, valleys, rivers, and brooks all running most pleasantly into a fair bay compassed, but for the mouth, with fruitful and delightsome land."

Parties of exploration pushed out gingerly on short trips, but it was late August before Smith, with Percy as his lieutenant, led a group of about a dozen men up the James River. They stopped frequently so Smith could make notes for his charts and maps, and several days passed before they came at last to the town of the Chickahominy.

Sentries had given notice of their impending arrival,

and the community looked deserted when the shallop swept around a bend in the river. But Smith sensed that he was being watched, and directing the boat to head toward the bank, he reached into a sack and threw handfuls of inexpensive necklaces and other trinkets ashore.

The gestures were obviously peaceful, so a party of senior warriors came forward, and the visitors were escorted to the long house of the Council, where Powhatan awaited them. Initial communications were in sign language, but Smith had a flair for languages, and by the time the visit ended he was making rapid progress in speaking and understanding the tongue of the Chickahominy. He learned there were three other major rivers in the domain of the Chief of Chiefs, the Pamaunke, the Rappahannock and the Potomac. One of these rivers, Smith felt certain, inevitably led to the Pacific Ocean, which he believed to be only a short distance away.

Gifts were exchanged in gestures of mutual esteem, Smith and Percy presenting their hosts with several iron cooking pots, which Powhatan was quick to appreciate. In return the Englishmen received several loaves of unleavened corn bread and a number of full gourds of kernels, Powhatan indicating that although the season was advanced, it might not be too late to plant the grain. Smith immediately recognized the corn, which was found only in the New World, from descriptions written by Spanish explorers, who had called it maize, a corruption of a Carib Indian word, *mahis*. Refusing to be outdone in generosity, the gallant Captain presented Powhatan with a double-bladed smallsword.

Percy, who kept a gossipy *Journal* for the edification and entertainment of his family and friends, made no mention of any meeting with Powhatan's lovely daughter. Two other members of the party, who were literate and corresponded with relatives, made no mention of any such encounter in their letters, either.

Most important of all, Smith himself said not one word about Pocahontas in any of the three books he subsequently wrote about his experiences: *True Relation; A Map of Virginia with a Description of the Country;* and the *Generall*

Historie of Virginia. It is difficult to believe that either he or Percy, both of them notoriously susceptible to feminine charms, would have failed to record a meeting with a girl subsequently hailed as a great beauty by all Englishmen.

Even if Pocahontas had not been hidden from view in the long house of the maidens, it is inconceivable that she would have been present during the visit of Smith, Percy and their comrades. All Chickahominy women habitually absented themselves from conclaves and meetings with strangers, particularly those whose ultimate aims and intentions had not been revealed.

Smith continued upstream on his voyage of exploration, finding the river navigable for a considerable distance. Above the falls, however, it became much narrower, so he reluctantly concluded he had not found a passage to the Pacific. Retracing his steps, he returned to Jamestown; by now it was too late in the season to plant the corn.

One of the tragedies of Jamestown's early days was the election of Wingfield as the first President of the Council. As amply illustrated in his own book, *Discourse of America*, written after he eventually returned to England, Wingfield lacked the personal elasticity and the understanding to realize that it would not be possible to re-create an English village on the shores of Virginia, but that survival depended upon the ability of the colonists to adapt themselves to the wilderness and develop a new type of civilization. Like most of his colleagues, the new President believed the Indians should be shunned whenever possible and forced to keep their distance. Only John Smith and Commodore Newport were wise enough to perceive that the newcomers could learn many things from the Chickahominy about New World living conditions and how to cope with them.

But Smith, excluded from the Council, had no active voice in the administration of the colony's affairs. And Newport, although influential, was not a permanent member of the community; he would return to England as soon as it was convenient for him to leave. The real miracle of Jamestown is that it did survive.

Instead of devoting their first efforts to the building of solid houses that would give them shelter from the autumn rains and the cold of winter, the colonists concentrated on the task of constructing high palisades of sharpened logs around a perimeter, then putting up a fort and emplacing their cannon. Wingfield engaged in petty disputes with Archer and Gosnold, and lacked the strength to stop the gentlemen-adventurers from engaging in quarrels over matters of no significance.

Smith sensibly refused to be a party to these feuds, and instead went off on a longer trip of exploration, taking Percy and Archer as his lieutenants, along with a small company of men. Several accounts of their journey later found their way into print, the best and most widely read being Smith's own *True Relation.* Another, written by Percy, was published sixteen years later. Unfortunately, this document was edited by the Reverend Samuel Purchas, an English clergyman who imagined himself Archdeacon Hakluyt's successor, but who had no discernible talent for the various tasks he set himself. Unable to differentiate between fact and fancy, he spoiled whatever might have been valuable in Percy's narrative by inept editing. The third account was a *Journal* written by Archer, but this man of action was so lacking in perceptivity that his diary was prosaic and uninformative.

The party frequently encountered bands of warriors from various tribes of the Chickahominy Confederation, and occasionally the Englishmen paid visits to Indian villages. Smith, who was impatient in his dealings with his fellow countrymen and could be brutal to those who stood in his path, displayed remarkable delicacy in his treatment of the Indians. He was gentle and patient, always good-humored. He unfailingly handed out gifts and he worked hard to learn the language of the natives. Within a relatively few months he could converse with almost all of the Indians he encountered, and had no difficulty in making himself understood or comprehending what they said to him.

When the explorers moved into the interior, Powhatan gave them his own younger son, Piaoko, as a guide. Perhaps Smith learned of Pocahontas's existence from her brother, but if that is the case he failed to record it in *True Relation* or elsewhere. He did write in detail about the feasts served by his hosts in various villages, the principal meals consisting of roasted venison, a stew of porcupine and oysters cooked in their shells on hot stones. He also mentioned a porridge of coarsely pounded cornmeal and water, to which a syrup made of the sap of maple trees was added. This syrup was so sweet, he declared, that he and his companions almost gagged on it, but the Indians who served the dish seemed addicted to it.

Smith was surprised to discover that one tribe grew small quantities of wheat, coarser than that of England or the Continent. It was used not to make bread, however, but primarily to thicken stews. The strawberries and mulberries were superior to those of the Old World, and Smith encountered another berry that was new to him. It had a deep blue color and smooth skin, was deliciously sweet and temporarily stained the teeth of anyone who ate it. He called it a blueberry, and in *True Relation* he heartily recommended it to his compatriots, saying it would become very popular if grown in the south of England.

Again traveling to the falls of the James River, Smith burned an inscription into a wooden cross, informing any bother Europeans who might reach the site that he was claiming all of the territory as far to the west as the Pacific Ocean in the name of King James. This innocent gesture later became a base for the English claims to much of the North American continent.

The weather was growing cooler as the party, in high spirits, leisurely made its way back to Jamestown. Upon their return, they were stunned to find the town a shambles. It had been subjected to a surprise attack twenty-four hours earlier by a tribe of Chesapeake Indians not associated with Powhatan's Chickahominy Confederation, and Wingfield had been totally unprepared for the assault. A man and a teen-aged boy had been killed, and a dozen other colonists had suffered injuries. The casualties would have been far worse had it not been for Captain Gosnold, who had rowed out to the anchored ships with a number of sailors and fired the cannon on board. The roar of the big guns had frightened the attackers, and they had fled without taking the loot that had been the object of their raid.

The outraged Smith insisted that a twenty-four-hour watch be maintained, that all members of the colony carry firearms wherever they went and that a new training program be instituted to improve the colony's defenses. His ideas were so sensible that the artisans clamored for his admission to the Council, and a majority of the members of that body now supported him. Smith was duly elected, and although Wingfield still held the title of President, it was the new member who took charge.

He, more than any other individual, was responsible for the survival of the community. First he built two high watchtowers and posted around-the-clock sentries in them. Then, again demonstrating his practical nature, he ordered the land cleared for several hundred feet in every direction from the palisades, which would make it impossible for the Chesapeake to launch another sneak attack on the colony.

Smith did not allow himself to forget what other members of the Council had ignored: the directors of the London Company expected Jamestown to show a profit. So the tallest and sturdiest trees of oak, maple, beech and white pine were felled and their trunks were sawed into prime lumber, then stored in the holds of the ships. Smith also concluded a barter deal with the Chickahominy, giving the Indians additional cooking utensils, blankets and other items in return for beaver and fox pelts. He obtained only a few bales of skins in the initial trade, but knew the sight of them would whet the appetites of the directors for more.

He also initiated a long-term project, the planting of the coarse tobacco that grew wild in the meadowlands of Virginia. The demand for snuff and pipe tobacco in England was already great and was increasing, and Smith believed that the "green gold," as he called it, could become a valuable product. The other members of the Council lacked his foresight, however, and the project languished because of their lack of interest in it.

Commodore Newport sailed off to England in the *Susan Constant*, his hold filled with the raw materials of the New World. The directors were disappointed because no gold or precious stones had been found, but they agreed to send two ships laden with provisions for the members of the colony who had remained behind, 105 men and boys in all.

The winter of 1607-8 was a nightmare for the residents of Jamestown. Their houses were "none too snug," as Smith later wrote, and they suffered severely from the cold and damp. Their supplies of wheat and barley were short, and only deals made by Smith with the Indians brought in enough corn, meat and oysters to prevent starvation.

Then, one by one, members of the colony fell ill. They suffered from an ailment they called "the sickness," and no one knew how to treat it. One moment a man was seemingly in good health, but suddenly he ran a high fever, a rash appeared on his body and he became too dizzy to stand. At least half of the colonists were bedded by the complaint, which forced the healthy to work that much harder.

Captain Bartholomew Gosnold was the first to die of "the sickness," and within three weeks forty-five others also expired. Captain Smith fell ill, but drank large quantities of cool water, and recovered within a few days. He insisted that others be treated in the same way, and saved the life of Captain Ratcliffe, among others, by forcing him to drink as much water as he could tolerate.

Wingfield bungled again by ordering that convalescents be given nothing to eat until they were strong enough to work. This rule was so absurd that the survivors of "the sickness" were on the verge of revolt, and a serious insurrection was prevented only by the combined efforts of Smith, Martin, Archer and Percy. A complete overhaul of the Council obviously was needed.

It was discovered that Kendal had been conspiring against the other gentlemen-adventurers, hoping to take complete charge while they were ill. The precise nature of the charges against him have never been made clear, but his colleagues regarded them so seriously that several wanted to shoot him on the spot. Smith and several others insisted he be given a trial, however, so he was placed under arrest and lodged under guard in an isolated hut.

Then Wingfield was deposed as President, and was sent out to the *Discovery*, a precaution taken to prevent the disgruntled members of the colony from murdering him. He was also ordered deported to England as soon as another ship that would return to London reached Virginia.

A new Council was formed, with only three men sharing the responsibility for the colony's administration: Smith, Ratcliffe and Martin. The improvement in Jamestown's fortunes began when they took office.

IX

The men and boys of Jamestown devoted themselves exclusively to hard work in the early spring of 1608. Crops of corn, wheat, barley, beans and peas were planted, and the first attempts were made to grow strawberries and blueberries. Fishing parties daily went out to sea in the *Discovery*, under the command of Captain Ratcliffe. New, stronger houses were built, and the thatched roofs of the original dwellings having proved inadequate, stout lumber was used as roofing. The fort was strengthened, new storehouses were built and work was started on the construction of a church.

Food for the next few months was the most pressing

need, so Captain Smith made his third trip to the main town of the Chickahominy, traveling in the shallop. He took along a quantity of the sharp metal axes the Indians had admired on their visit to Jamestown, hoping to barter them for parched corn and smoked meat.

Presumably it was on this trip that Smith and Powhatan fell out, and the Englishman's life was alleged to have been saved by Pocahontas, who successfully begged her father to spare him. If Smith was on bad terms with the Chief of Chiefs, he did not mention that fact in either the *True Relation* or the *Generall Historie*. It has already been noted that the name of Pocahontas did not appear in either of these books. No other account of the colony's early days mentioned any quarrel, much less the name of Pocahontas. Wingfield, who was already working on his book while awaiting transportation to England, damned his former colleagues unmercifully, and would have relished the inclusion of an item about Smith, a member of the group that had deposed him from office. But he says nothing about the matter, either.

In both of his major works mentioning this journey to the interior, Smith boasted in some detail of the success he enjoyed. He and his companions returned to Jamestown with thirty bushels of corn, twenty of wheat and seventeen of "coarse Indian rye, too strong in taste for bread, but nourishing when made into a paste with water, baked and eaten with the gum of the maple tree." They brought back sides of venison and bear bacon, wildfowl, fish, oysters and sacks filled with salt from a deer lick, the first they had obtained, which made it possible for them, thereafter, to preserve fresh game, fowl and fish.

The finding of the deer lick, Smith wrote in both of his books, was the single most important consequence of the trip. It made the colonists independent of provisions of salt brought from England, enabled them to institute a systematic process of storing food for future use and allowed them to hope, for the first time, that the colony would not founder. Never one to refrain for an instant from discussing personal experiences, Smith could not have "forgotten" the supposed saving of his life by Pocahontas. What concerned him was the deer lick, and he was correct in his evaluation of its benefits.

The colonists tended their crops assiduously, and reaped gratifyingly large harvests of corn, peas and beans, the wheat and barley faring less well. It was during the spring, summer and autumn of 1608 that the Englishmen seriously began to adapt themselves to the New World. The clothes they had brought with them on their expedition were wearing out, so they learned to cure deerskin and the tougher hide of the buffalo that roamed the valleys of the interior. By the late autumn almost everyone was wearing shirts, trousers and moccasins made of rawhide.

Most firearms were blunderbusses, short guns with wide muzzles that were notoriously inaccurate. It was difficult to shoot game with them, unless one was an extraordinary shot, and since only Smith, Archer and Percy were good enough shots to kill game, the colony continued to depend on the Indians for most of their meat supplies. Blunderbusses were useless in bringing down wildfowl, so the men of Jamestown adopted the Chickahominy system of snaring ducks, geese and turkeys. There were almost unlimited quantities of oysters, crabs and clams for the taking, and everyone became tired of fish. Mussels were regarded as great delicacies, and clams, unknown in England and Continental Europe, later came to be called "the American caviar."

Violence flared again when Kendal was transferred to the *Discovery* because it was deemed wiser to keep him there, and he began to plot with Wingfield. The pair persuaded some crew members to sail back to England with them, but Ratcliffe and Smith learned of the plot in time and smashed the conspiracy. All of the plotters except Kendal and a sailor named Read surrendered. The pair put up armed resistance, but were overwhelmed, and subsequently were sentenced to death by the unanimous vote of all the gentlemen-adventurers in the colony. A gallows was erected, and they were hanged the next day.

Smith's journeys of exploration took him farther from Jamestown in the late autumn of 1608, and one of his adventures, about which he wrote in some detail, may have given him the idea for the claim he later made, under circumstances to be discussed in a subsequent chapter, that he had been the prisoner of Powhatan. He was exploring in the general vicinity of the area that would be known, two centuries later, as the District of Columbia, when he and his men were surrounded by a large band of Potomac warriors. Rather than use their firearms and cause bloodshed, which would have caused the Indians to retaliate against Jamestown, Smith directed his men to surrender quietly.

They were taken before a Sachem of the Potomac named Opechancanough, a chief of one of the Chickahominy nations with whom Powhatan had encountered difficulties on occasion. The Indian wanted Smith's pistols, and when the Englishman refused to surrender them, his captor ordered him tied to a stake and stabbed to death. According to *True Relation* and the *Generall Historie,* Smith saved his life by showing the chief his compass, which fascinated the Indian. Other sources later confirmed the fact that Opechancanough became a good friend, visited Jamestown on a number of occasions and, prior to Smith's departure for England, was ceremoniously presented with an old pistol from which the hammer had been removed.

Other colonists were less fortunate than Smith in their encounters with Indians. A gentleman-adventurer, Jehu Robinson, was killed and scalped by unknown assailants while on a day-long hunting trip, and a carpenter, Thomas Emry, later suffered a similar fate. George Cassen, who had been a merchant seaman before becoming a member of the expedition, wandered away from Jamestown and was never seen again. It was assumed by everyone in the settlement, Smith included, that he had been captured by a band of unfriendly Chesapeake, and this story was later embroidered. In his *Generall Historie* Smith wrote that Cassen had been killed by slow torture, and offered his readers horrifying details. But others merely said that he vanished and was not seen again in Jamestown. It is possible that he lost his way in the forest and starved to death, or he might have met any one of a number of other fates. If he was indeed captured and tortured by a subtribe of the Chesapeake, only Smith knew it.

In the autumn of 1608 Commodore Newport returned to Jamestown in the *Susan Constant,* the ship's hold filled with provisions of every kind, from munitions to food to blankets, along with various small luxury items the colonists had not seen in a long time. There were eighty recruits for the settlement on board, all of them healthy, and forty more were expected on board another ship, the *Phoenix*, commanded by Captain Francis Nelson, which was to arrive within a few days. The newcomers breathed life into Jamestown when it most needed a transfusion. The total population had dropped to thirty-eight persons prior to Newport's return.

A week later a new catastrophe struck. A fire broke out in one of the thatched cottages hastily built for the new arrivals, and spread to other parts of the settlement. No one was killed, but several houses were burned, and the Reverend Mr. Hunt's precious library was totally destroyed. One portion of the fort was damaged, and as soon as it was repaired the Council ordered a church fit for religious services contructed before any more houses were raised. The entire community took part, and the church was built in less than a week.

Among the new arrivals were three gentlemen-adventurers of stature and ability: the Phettiplace brothers, William and Michael, were industrious and dependable, and Matthew Scrivener, who was given a seat on the Council at the direction of the London Company's directors, probably was the most energetic and sensible of Jamestown's early settlers, excluding only John Smith.

The *Phoenix* did not appear, and was presumed lost. Newport remained in the colony until the following April, delaying his departure until he could collect enough furs to satisfy the demands of the directors. When he departed he gave Wingfield passage to England and, at the suggestion of the Council, also took the overly-ambitious Gabriel Archer with him. A scant day after the *Susan Constant* sailed, President Ratcliffe lost a hand while cleaning his fowling piece, and for the rest of his term he was a very sick man. The full burden of administration fell on Smith, who relied on Martin and Scrivener for help.

His first crisis came sooner than expected. The new members of the community, who had been led to believe the New World was a modern paradise, mutinied and refused to work. Captain Smith took the leaders into custody, threatening to hang any man who did not go to his appointed place of work without delay, and the mutiny ended.

Late in April the missing *Phoenix* finally reached Jamestown, and the bluff Captain Nelson revealed he had spent a long sojourn in the West Indian islands. His cargo was intact because his passengers and crew had obtained all they wanted to eat and drink by bartering personal effects with the natives. And the deck of the *Phoenix* was heaped high with tunny, the ship having sailed through a school of the huge fish the previous day. The entire community, including the newest settlers just arrived on the *Phoenix*, went to work salting the tuna and storing it in the warehouses for the long months ahead.

Thereafter the newcomers learned the ways of the wilderness from the veterans, and Smith spent all of his spare time working on *A True Relation*. As he explained in a preface, his purpose in writing the book was to give the people an unvarnished account of New World life. It annoyed him when immigrants had to be disabused of the notion that precious metals and stones could be found everywhere. Trying to encourage immigration on a realistic basis, he glossed over the Council feuds that had caused so much trouble, and unlike Wingfield, whose *Discourse of America* was published at approximately the same time, he attacked none of his colleagues.

He also wrote a number of long reports for Archdeacon Hakluyt, enclosing many maps, charts and sketches, and prepared some maps of the North American coastline, basing them on what he had learned from Gosnold. These maps were used by Henry Hudson on his voyages of discovery a few years later.

The manuscript for the book and the other written matter were given to Captain Nelson when he returned to England, and Prince Henry assumed financial responsibility for publication of the *True Relation*. One of the last maps Smith drew was a large, astonishingly accurate representation of Chesapeake Bay. This work, together with Smith's detailed description of the area, was published in 1612, and assured him of a permanent place in the ranks of the foremost North American explorers.

Many of the newcomers fell ill of "the sickness," but all were forced to drink large quantities of water, and not one died. Veterans who had survived their earlier attack of the ailment appeared to be immune.

Ratcliffe was unable to function as the head of the government, but was reluctant to give up the office. The other gentlemen-adventurers felt something had to be done, however, and threatened to turn him out of office unless he offered his voluntary resignation. Ratcliffe took the hint and vacated the office.

On July 21 Captain John Smith was unanimously elected to the post he had held in all but name, and became President of Virginia and of the King's Council there. Matthew Scrivener was named his deputy.

Scrivener's election enabled Smith to keep up his trips of exploration, and he made a long journey into what later became Pennsylvania, where he mapped the Susquehanna River and its environs. He carried no cartographer's tools, using only his quill pen and sheets of paper, and he did work that could not be improved upon for more than a century and a half. Subsequently he was the first to set foot on the site of what would become the city of Norfolk, and traveled a distance up the Elizabeth River.

His duties to Jamestown were never forgotten, and at Norfolk he established friendly relations with members of a small, independent tribe of Indians, the Nansemond. They presented him with four hundred baskets filled with corn and "so many bales of dried venison that the shallop sat low in the water." Not the least of the functions Smith performed was that of accumulating vast stores of knowledge about the New World, especially the best ways to treat the Indians, and he explained all he discovered in his books. Generations that followed were permanently in his debt.

Under Smith's administration Jamestown flourished for the first time, and he proved—to the satisfaction of the Crown, the directors of the London Company and, above all, the British public—that it was indeed possible to establish a permanent, viable colony in the New World. His methods were somewhat dictatorial, and the colonists were given no voice in their own government, but he succeeded without violating the sacred personal liberties of all Englishmen.

Solid new dwellings and warehouses were built, orderly

streets were laid out, and the settlers were encouraged to sell any products they themselves made, including woodcarvings, in a small shop located a short distance from the church, which boasted a steeple by the early months of 1609. A second, higher wall was built around the town, and land was cleared far beyond the fields in which grain and vegetables were grown. It might be noted that after Smith's first rebuff at the hands of the Council he made no new attempts to grow tobacco.

Formal military drills were held every Sunday, after worship services, in a clearing that came to be known as Smith Field, and although the Captain's little "army" could not have gone to war against professional soldiers, they impressed the Indians who sometimes came to watch the colonists march, maneuver and shoot their blunderbusses. When there were visitors, Smith made certain his men fired at targets large enough to hit.

A perfectionist in matters of defense, Smith was dissatisfied with the fort, which was triangular in shape. He had learned that the Indians always used the element of surprise in their attacks, and he minimized that technique by designing a new, star-shaped fort with five points. It would be simple, he declared, to give flank support with muskets to any portion of the building under attack.

He drew a sketch for a new fort, and the colonists built it under Scrivener's careful supervision. Smith's design proved so successful that it was later copied by other settlements and eventually became standard throughout Britain's American colonies, from New England to Georgia, until the outbreak of the War of Independence one hundred and fifty years later.

Most colonists were so exhausted by the end of the day that they went to bed soon after eating their supper, but Smith, endowed with almost superhuman energy, went to work on a new project, *A Map of Virginia, with a Description of the Country*. He had been thinking of contemporaries when writing the *True Relation*, but he prepared his new work with posterity in mind. His details were painstakingly accurate, and he hoped *A Map of Virginia* would win him lasting fame, which it did.

Smith noted in this work that twenty-eight of the new

members of the community died within a few months of their arrival, but not one of the veterans fell ill. This led him to the conclusion that the longer a man remained in America, the more immune he became to the perils of nature. A little more than a decade later the Pilgrims, who settled in what became New England, made the same observation.

Late in the year the *Susan Constant* arrived again, bringing still more colonists and ever-welcome supplies. Two gentlemen-adventurers, Richard Waldo and Peter Winne, were given places on the Council at the order of the London Company's directors. Both were men of stature who proved their worth.

Two of the new arrivals were women, the first to come to the colony, and the days of an exclusively male settlement came to an end for all time. One was a Mistress Forest, who is believed to have been the wife of Thomas Forest, a gentleman-adventurer, but may have been married to his kinsman, George Forest. Nothing more is known about her.

The other was her maidservant, a girl of about twenty years named Anne Burrowes, whom Smith described as "lively, intelligent and modest." About a year after her arrival she was married, in a ceremony conducted by the Reverend Mr. Hunt, to John Laydon, a member of the original expedition who had come to the New World as a common laborer and became an expert farmer. Their sons owned small plantations and their grandsons became wealthy tobacco growers. The unassuming Anne was the founder of a long, aristocratic line.

The presence of two women in the colony caused a startling change. Men became more careful of their appearance, and Captain Smith promised a jail sentence to anyone who cursed in public. Other men sent for their sweethearts, and at Smith's suggestion the London Company eventually sent out a boatload of unmarried women who wanted husbands and a life in the New World. The presence of the women meant that English colonists had come to the New World to stay.

Commodore Newport also brought Smith a letter from the directors of the Company that showed their total ignorance of the New World. After castigating him for his "failure" to send back gold, silver and precious stones, they ordered him to "crown" Powhatan in an appropriate ceremony and to obtain from him a pledge of allegiance to his "higher monarch," King James I.

The directors also sent another, equally maddening order. A number of Polish and Dutch immigrants were on board the *Susan Constant*, and Smith was told to utilize their services in a "factory" making glass and tar, as there was a demand for these products in England. Apparently it was impossible for high-born nobles sitting in London to realize that the services of every newcomer were desperately needed in agricultural work, fishing and hunting.

Smith and Newport paid a visit to Powhatan, who had no use for the gilded crown they gave him, but liked the handsome cape of scarlet wool, lined in silk. What he thought of the personal gift sent him by his "brother monarch and liege lord," James, is unknown. It was a four-poster bed, complete with a feather-stuffed mattress, the first ever seen in America. The bed vanished from history as soon as it appeared, and no one knows to what use it might have been put. In return the gracious Powhatan sent King James two beaver pelts and a handsome lynx hide.

When Smith told his host of James's request for an oath of allegiance, he took care to address the Chief of Chiefs in rapid-fire English which Powhatan did not understand. That ended the matter; Smith had done his duty, Powhatan was none the wiser and no one was harmed.

Both Smith and Newport reported the incident in their private correspondence, the latter firmly indicating to friends in England that it would have been suicidal for either to mention King James's absurd demand to an Indian potentate who had never heard of him and had no reason to bow to any other man alive.

There was no reference in the letters of either to Pocahontas, much less to the saving of Smith's life. It should be remembered that Pocahontas was still living in the long house of the maidens, and Smith had no greater opportunity to become acquainted with her than he had on his previous visits to the town of the Chickahominy.

The other orders of the directors could not be ignored

with equal impunity, so the entire community went to work making glass and tar, which were loaded in the hold of the *Susan Constant*. There was also a demand in London for something called "red root," which supposedly had powerful medicinal properties. The colonists had discovered it was worthless, but the directors were so insistent in their demand for large quantities of it that Smith went off on a five-day trip to the opposite end of Chesapeake Bay to obtain several bags of the root from Indians who must have found his request puzzling.

Before the *Susan Constant* sailed again, Smith wrote a hard-headed letter to the directors of the London Company. Patiently explaining that there were no precious metals and stones in the portion of North America that England was claiming, he enclosed a number of rock samples to prove his point. But the riches of the New World were far greater than the wealthy London nobles imagined. He extolled the wonders of nature he had seen, lovingly described the wilderness and went into detail about the rich soil, the climate that was beneficial to colonists and, above all, the opportunity to create an empire there.

He enclosed copies of the comprehensive maps he had made of Virginia and Chesapeake Bay, and he also wrote in detail about the navigability of rivers, the natural obstacles that had to be overcome and the traits of the various Indian tribes he had encountered. In a separate packet he sent a number of maps to his friend Henry Hudson, who received the valuable documents on the eve of his departure from England to enter the employ of the Dutch.

Most of Smith's letter to the directors was devoted to a criticism of the type of immigrants being sent to Jamestown. Many were physically and temperamentally unable to live in the wilderness and were a liability to the colony. What Virginia needed, he declared, were gardeners, farmers, carpenters, fishermen, stonemasons, blacksmiths and "fellows with strong backs and hands who will dig up the root-stumps of trees."

Courageous men had already performed miracles, Smith said, but the hazards of day-to-day living were increasing. The total population of Jamestown now numbered more than two hundred, and it was inevitable that there would be friction between the English settlers, the Poles and the Dutch. It would be difficult to obtain food for so many people from the Indians, and the colony was not yet self-sufficient in its production of grains and vegetables. Therefore the failure of a single year's crops could cause disaster. In order to avert catastrophe, the directors were urged to send four supply ships immediately.

Had all of Smith's recommendations been followed, the growth of the colony would have been remarkable. But the directors still had many lessons to learn, and the colonists were doomed to suffer many additional hardships before their future became secure and Virginia lived up to her bright promise.

X

The Nansemond agreed to sell Jamestown regularly delivered supplies of meat and corn, but they could not meet the colony's increased demand, and Captain Smith was forced to turn to the Chickahominy for help. The situation was delicate. Powhatan had watched the establishment of the English settlement with equanimity, but was certain to become apprehensive about his own security as the colony continued to grow. Even now, although the Chief of Chiefs did not quite realize it, two hundred Englishmen and Europeans armed with fowling pieces, pistols and cannon were more than a match for an army of braves many times their number.

91

A new trade agreement was made, Piaoko coming to Jamestown to negotiate the terms, but Smith deliberately asked for far less than he actually needed. It is also significant that it was Piaoko rather than his father who was invited to Jamestown for talks. As far as is known, Powhatan himself did not visit the colony during the first years of its existence. At least there is no mention of any such visit in the books written about Virginia's first days or in the correspondence of the literate colonists.

Certainly this situation suited Smith and his Council. They did not want the powerful Chief of Chiefs to evaluate the colony with his own eyes, to become aware of Jamestown's growing strength or of her vulnerability. Only when the settlement became too strong to be dislodged by Chickahominy force would Powhatan be a welcome guest.

For the present it was enough that the Confederation tribes sold the colony limited quantities of food, and that warriors were coming to Jamestown to barter for the bales of beaver, fox, lynx and other furs. Occasionally a settler and an individual brave might quarrel, but relations with Powhatan remained tranquil, and the Council wanted nothing to disturb the peace.

Smith suffered a severe blow when Matthew Scrivener was drowned, and the entire colony felt the loss of the deputy leader. Some of the newer gentlemen-adventurers were competent, honest men, but there was none Smith could trust as much, and discipline was tightened.

Twenty-two new houses were built during the winter of 1609–10, and the church was given a new, badly needed roof. An assembly hall was built, reflecting the growing needs of the community, and permanent offices were established there for the President and members of his Council. Three new wells were dug, much to the relief of the whole community, and everyone rejoiced when the water proved to be sweet. For two and one-half years the entire colony had been complaining that the drinking water had a metallic taste. During bad weather, when outdoor work could not be performed, the men made fishnets of vines similar to those used by the coastal Indian tribes.

The food situation continued to improve, thanks in

part to the pigs and chickens that had been a part of Commodore Newport's last cargo. The pig and chicken population grew rapidly, eggs were available in quantity for the first time, and fears of starvation began to recede.

Smith maintained his policy of open-handed generosity to the Indians, and sent Powhatan a gift of two hammers and a keg of nails, dispatching with them several sketches showing how a house could be built in the style Jamestown preferred to the crude huts of the Chickahominy. Whether Powhatan ever utilized the gift and his braves built him an English-style house is not known.

Early in the winter another merchant ship reached Jamestown under the command of Captain Samuel Argall. He was a burly man with red hair and beard and small black eyes so intense that their effect was almost hypnotic. Argall was totally lacking in tact, spoke his mind bluntly and was prepared to defend his opinions with his sword. Some of the early authors who told the Pocahontas story tended to portray Argall as a villain, a cunning and unscrupulous man endowed with a streak of cruelty.

They probably went too far in their condemnation of him. A more dispassionate study of Argall indicates that he was impetuous, that his horizons were limited and that, like so many self-made men, he thought his own way of handling a given situation was preferable to any other. His alleged brutality is a matter of conjecture, but he managed to maintain peaceful relations with Smith, who could not abide bullies, so it well may be that Argall was not as black as he has been painted.

Argall brought letters with him that indicated a major change in the future of Virginia. King James had become personally interested in the project and had directed his Privy Council to insure its growth, security and well-being. A fleet of nine large ships was being prepared for a voyage to Virginia, and between five and six hundred new colonists, including both men and women, soon would sail for Jamestown. In years to come they would be followed by many others, the traveling expenses of all immigrants to be paid by the Crown.

It was obvious that a vastly expanded colony would need a new type of government, so one of the most competent directors of the London Company was coming to the New World to become the Royal Governor. He was Thomas West, Lord de la Warr, a distinguished soldier, able administrator and strict disciplinarian. He would be accompanied by his wife, one of England's loveliest and most charming ladies, and her presence in Jamestown would mean that a viceregal court in miniature would be established there.

A large staff would come to the New World, too, each of its members bearing an imposing title. Sir George Somers, knight, a rear admiral in the Royal Navy who was as agile in promoting his own interests at court as he was competent at sea, would become Admiral of the New World Fleet. Sir Thomas Dale, a baronet whose family was influential at court, would be the High Marshal, a post that would combine the duties of military commander-in-chief with those of a police chief. Sir Thomas was an amiable man who had seen limited military service, and there were those at Whitehall who snickered when they learned of his appointment, but he would prove himself a courageous and hard-working deputy to Lord de la Warr. One Sir Ferdinando Wainman, a knight, would hold the resounding title of General of Horse, but it was difficult to picture his duties because there were no horses in the colony and none were being sent. Commodore Newport would return permanently to the New World, too, and would become Vice Admiral of the Fleet.

Several of Jamestown's original colonists, who had gone back to England, were returning to live in Jamestown again. Archer, Ratcliffe and Martin were specifically mentioned in the dispatches.

Captain John Smith, who had done so much for Jamestown, would remain in office, technically, as President only until Baron de la Warr arrived, although Smith left Jamestown before de la Warr came there, at which time he would retire to private life and his Council would be disbanded. He was given no position in the new government, the Crown offered him no recognition for the services he had performed and if he elected to remain in Virginia it would be in the capacity of a private citizen. Smith makes no mention of his demotion in his *Generall Historie*, but he was a vain, proud man and must have been deeply hurt by King James's neglect.

A hurricane scattered the ships of the squadron in the vicinity of Bermuda, forcing several to land there. Late in the year five of the vessels finally reached Jamestown, their supplies virtually exhausted and their passengers sick. The arrival of several hundred helpless, ill men and women severely strained the facilities of the colony, and as Lord de la Warr's ship was not among the arrivals, Smith was forced to cope with the situation.

He did his best, even though Garbriel Archer tried to have him dismissed at once as President. Married couples were assigned houses, every able-bodied man went to work building more dwellings, and emissaries went to every Indian tribe in the area, offering a variety of goods in exchange for food. Many of the Indians yearned for the fire sticks of the foreigners, and some said they would not trade unless they received guns, but Smith long had maintained a policy of refusing to sell firearms to the Indians under any circumstances, and he refused to reverse himself now, even though the situation appeared desperate.

It was obvious that Jamestown would have to produce much more of her own food in the years to come, so Smith did not wait for the arrival of Lord de la Warr and tried to anticipate the need himself. He sent a party of one hundred persons some miles inland to establish what he called plantations. The area he selected was a fertile meadowland where it would be necessary to uproot only a few trees. Each of the colonists would be assigned his own fields to cultivate, but for the present all would live in a blockhouse the men would construct.

Jamestown's spread into the interior involved the risk of arousing Powhatan's ire and starting a war with the whole Chickahominy Confederation, but Smith rightly believed that he had no choice. He would have preferred a more gradual policy of expansion, but he had been given no voice in the matter, and it was obvious that a Jamestown of approximately eight hundred inhabitants would need to grow crops on a scale far larger than any yet attempted.

A short time after the new outpost was established Smith went up the James River in his shallop on an inspection trip. He made suggestions, remained overnight and the following morning started back to Jamestown. Most of the men accompanying him had adopted the Indian habit of smoking pipes, and one of them accidentally set fire to Smith's gunpowder bag with a tinderbox and flint. There was a flash of fire, and John Smith was enveloped in flames.

He leaped overboard, thereby saving his life, but was so badly burned he was incapacitated. In the days that followed it became obvious that he needed medical treatment unavailable in the New World, but he refused to leave until Lord de la Warr arrived and officially succeeded him. His condition failed to improve, however, and he finally agreed to leave for England on board the *Unity*, the first of the ships to sail to England. He left Jamestown late in November, 1609, and never again saw the colony to which he had given his talents, devotion and energies.

Conditions in Jamestown became chaotic after Smith's departure, and in the absence of leadership, the food situation, which had looked so promising for the winter of 1609–10, deteriorated rapidly. Stores were depleted because the colonists lacked the foresight to accept rationing, and there was no one of stature on hand to deal with the Indians. Statistics are difficult to obtain, but it is believed that, out of a population of more than five hundred persons, as many as four hundred or more may have died that winter, which became known as "the starving time."

It is in accounts of this winter that the name of Pocahontas is mentioned by people other than Captain John Smith. According to Percy, a twelve-year old boy named Henry Spelman, the youngest son of Sir Henry Spelman, a noted English scholar, became so hungry that he wandered far inland in search of food, was taken into custody by the Chickahominy and would have been killed by Powhatan, for unknown reasons, but was saved by the intervention of Pocahontas.

Early in 1614 Spelman returned to London and related his experience in a little pamphlet, *An Account of the Starving Time in Virginia.* It was published late in 1614, and attracted little attention, but well may have been read by Captain Smith, who went to great pains to keep himself informed of everything that took place in Jamestown.

The most significant feature of Spelman's own story is that it differed in detail from Percy's, and from the story later told by Smith. According to the boy himself, he was treated with great kindness by Pocahontas—now a "graduate" of the long house of the maidens—and by her father. Spelman at no time indicates that his life was endangered or that Pocahontas had to intervene with her father to protect him. Percy, like Smith, was not content to accept a simple story, but felt compelled to embellish and dramatize it.

Certainly there was no reason for Powhatan to have condemned young Spelman to death or to have threatened him in any way. Smith and other English leaders had paid sporadic visits to the main town of the Chickahominy in the past, just as Piaoko and other braves had visited Jamestown, so the boy's sudden appearance was no novelty. Even if it were argued that Powhatan was becoming upset by the increase in the size of the neighboring community whose presence he had tolerated for two and a half years, he could have chosen many effective ways to make his wrath known. The execution of a harmless boy would have impressed no one, and could have given the Chief of Chiefs little satisfaction, either. So Spelman's own version of his mild adventure must be taken at face value, while the taller tale told by Percy is suspect.

In any event, Lord de la Warr, Sir Thomas Gates and Sir George Somers finally reached Jamestown in the early spring of 1610, accompanied by more than one hundred and fifty settlers. The provisions they carried ended the "starving time," and thereafter other ships came to the colony at regular intervals, bringing food, supplies of all kinds and still more immigrants. De la Warr quickly justified the confidence shown in him by the Crown and his fellow London Company directors, and a new era in Jamestown's development and rapid growth was inaugurated.

Pocahontas was fated to pay her first visit to Jamestown later in 1610, but before proceeding to an account of her sojourn there it is well to see what became of Captain Smith in the years after he left Virginia.

Smith recovered his health in England, and although he was totally ignored by the directors of the London Company, *A True Relation*, published in 1610, created something of a sensation. It earned Smith large sums of money and made him famous; it also gave extensive publicity to the new colony and made it far easier for the London Company to recruit more immigrants.

Smith resumed an old affair with Frances, Duchess of Richmond, but he had fallen in love with America, and thereafter, for the rest of his life, the New World was ever-present in his mind. A series of meetings with Archdeacon Hakluyt, who eagerly accepted his maps and accounts, led to a session or two with Henry, Prince of Wales, and in time Smith was summoned to Whitehall to tell King James about the colony in which the monarch was now interested.

Like most men who were called to the palace for an audience with King James, Smith could not have enjoyed the experience. The monarch was a long-faced man with a lugubrious manner, his face usually concealed behind a handkerchief because he suffered from a perennial head cold. It was small wonder that he could not be cured: Whitehall was icy, and not even the luxurious tapestries that lined the stone walls could keep out the chill.

James was a parsimonious man who remembered a poverty-stricken childhood, and to him the burning of huge logs in the palace hearths was an outrageous expense. So the fires were feeble in apartments he occupied, and it was said, only half in jest, that the coldest chamber in the kingdom was the throne room. It was so chilly there that men were permitted to wear hats over their wigs, while ladies who followed current fashions and wore low-cut gowns would use any excuse to avoid making an appearance there. Only James, Queen Anne and the two princes were permitted to sit, although the Duke of Buckingham and other royal favorites were sometimes given the privilege.

The King ate frugally, and those who dined with him usually left the table hungry. Royal stewards watered the wine, and James was known to frown at anyone who consumed more than a glass or two. He did not object to spirits as such, however, provided someone else paid for them.

John Smith was a robust, lusty man who found it difficult to converse with the eccentric ruler, and regarded the audience as a failure. But James, later called "the wisest fool in Christendom," was a better judge of character than most of his contemporaries realized, and Smith subsequently obtained his reward.

He published *A Map of Virginia, with a Description of the Country* in 1612, and it enjoyed a success equal to that of his first book. Smith was an authority on the New World, and was consulted by merchants interested in the expanding market there as well as by nobles interested in duplicating the success of the London Company. General interest in exploration was heightened by Henry Hudson's exploits, and everyone in England was conscious of the New World.

The directors of the London Company, who had been offended by Smith's blunt letter before he had left office as President of Virginia, found it expedient to make their peace with him. He could have returned to the colony in an official capacity, but Lord de la Warr was doing a first-rate job, and Smith's dignity prevented him from accepting any post other than that of Governor.

There was considerable speculation about the portion of North America north of Virginia, particularly the land that might lie beyond a "paradise" Bartholomew Gosnold had discovered in 1602 and had named Martha's Vineyard. Speculation was heightened by the discovery of a great river by Henry Hudson, and Smith found backing for an expedition of his own from several of the directors of the London Company, acting in a private capacity.

Accompanying him in his two ships were a pair of Indians previously brought to England by an expedition sponsored by the Earl of Southampton, and they readily agreed to act as Smith's guides in return for passage to their homes. He kept his word, and one of the most bizarre incidents in history was the result. One of the Indians died soon after he returned home, but the other survived, and in 1620, when the Pilgrams who crossed the Atlantic in the *Mayflower* landed in the wilderness they were to call New Plymouth, they were greeted by an Indian wearing a tattered English hat and speaking an English that was the broad cockney of London's lower classes. That Indian, known as Squanto, served the Pilgrims faithfully for many years and won his own place in American history.

Smith set out for the New World on March 3, 1614, with two ships, the *Frances* and the *Queen Anne*. Drawing accurate maps of the North American coastline from Nova Scotia and New Brunswick to Rhode Island, he carefully charted the estuaries of Maine's great rivers, the Penobscot and the Kennebec, and first went ashore at what became the site of Portsmouth, New Hampshire. He discovered the Merrimack River in Massachusetts, and spent several days with the Massachusetts Indians in their village at a place that would be known as Boston. He named the entire area New England, and called a Massachusetts river the Charles after King James's younger son. There were so many fish in the waters off a horn-shaped peninsula to the south that he named it Cape Cod, and he thought the waters of Rhode Island's Narragansett Bay comprised the mouth of the largest river on the continent.

Returning to England in triumph after a voyage that had lasted six months, he sold the furs and lumber he had obtained and actually made a profit on the voyage. Archdeacon Hakluyt eagerly accepted his superb maps and other data, and King James gave him the title of Admiral of New England. He held that honorary rank to the end of his days, but continued to call himself Captain John Smith.

In 1615 he set out again on a voyage to the New World, but his capture by a French privateer disrupted his plans. In 1616 he brought out his third book, *A Description of New England.* It was as successful as his earlier works, but Smith wanted more than stature as an author. He was eager to resume his explorations, but found that the wealthy nobles were reluctant to give him funds after his failure the previous year. He immediately launched a campaign to raise money, and pursued it with such vigor that many nobles came to regard him as a nuisance and closed their doors to him.

So, in spite of his various successes as an explorer and colonizer he was still an outsider when as will be seen, Pocahontas and her husband came to England.

XI

By the autumn of 1610 Jamestown had become a curious mixture of the Old World and the New. The recent arrivals from England, particularly the aristocrats, tried to cling to their London ways, but they fought a losing battle against the wilderness. Those who had been in America longer, particularly the hard-core group that had been members of the original party in 1607, preferred their adopted way of living. Most of the lower class newcomers, who made up the bulk of the population, sensibly emulated the veterans, yet all remained completely English at the same time.

The life of the "court" centered around Baron and

Lady de la Warr, who lived in an unpainted log and clapboard house of two stories. A few items of furniture, including their four-poster bed and a pair of matching divans, had come from England, but their chairs and tables were made by Jamestown carpenters. They used gourds for drinking cups and as receptacles for soups and stews, and their plates were smooth, square boards. Few paintings hung on the walls, and the floors were bare except in the sitting room and bedchamber, where they had placed the only Near Eastern rugs in all of North America. But Lord de la Warr's wine cellar was extensive, even though space in the holds of Jamestown-bound ships was badly needed for a large variety of products. De la Warr had been known in London for his fine clarets and burgundies, and he did not change his drinking habits.

There were three or four hundred books in the de la Warr library, but the Governor was too busy to read most of them, and eventually they found their way into the Reverend Mr. Hunt's restored library, which now occupied a building of its own. Precedent made it necessary for Lady de la Warr to set an example for the other women of the town, and she spent a portion of each day sewing and embroidering. Every afternoon she held open house, and any woman, regardless of her station, was welcome. In time she became the confidante and friend of many Jamestown women of a class she would never have met had she remained in London. She was also the arbiter of the colony's morals, and her judgments were final, perhaps because there was no one in America to whom her rulings could be appealed.

The demands of protocol prohibited the Governor and his lady from visiting the homes of others in the community, even those of the baronets and knights who were de la Warr's social equals and professional colleagues. So Lady de la Warr entertained frequently, and was said to be as good a conversationalist as the French, a high compliment from gentlemen-adventurers who habitually hated France.

In most respects the women were more advanced than their husbands and accepted New World customs or made their own more readily, but in matters of attire they remained more conservative. Every Jamestown man, even Lord de la Warr and his lieutenants, in time put away their fine English clothes and adopted the leather shirts, trousers and moccasins of America. But the women stubbornly continued to wear the long skirts, flowing sleeves and low-cut bodices of Whitehall and the London streets, a style of dress that was ill-suited to the wilderness, where women performed hard labor and frequently were required to do man's work.

However, they invented new dishes with gusto, experimented with local herbs and fruits and vegetables unknown in the Old World, and found appetizing ways to cook the corn, venison and fish that were the staples of their daily diet. They kept chickens, domesticated ducks, raised pigs. A reservoir for fish was dug, filled with water and stocked to their specifications. They grew flax and learned the art of spinning cloth, they boiled their soap and made their candles. They cultivated the wild plants of North America, and soon every home had its own vegetable garden, a necessity that was instrumental in preventing another time of starvation.

The men tamed the wilderness, cut down the forest to create their farms and continued to put up new buildings. The presence of increasing numbers of children caused the erection of a two-room schoolhouse in the autumn of 1610, and before the end of the year Jamestown boasted its first tavern, where ale, mead and wine could be purchased. The men had rejoiced when women had started coming to the colony, but being contrary creatures themselves, they had found it necessary to build a place to which they could escape.

Jamestown's attitude toward religion demonstrated the effect of the wilderness on Old World concepts. In the next half-century scores of colonies would be established by English minority groups trying to escape the persecutions that beset them at home, and they struggled valiantly to worship as they pleased, often excluding from their colony those who did not share the beliefs of the majority. But in Jamestown the opposite took place.

The first settlers in Virginia were devout Church of England members, as were most of those who followed them. No issues were raised over questions of faith, and it was taken for granted that the Reverend Mr. Hunt would conduct Anglican services. The coming of the Poles and Dutch immediately established two religious minority groups,

Roman Catholics and Dutch Reformed Protestants, but at no time were men of those faiths forbidden to worship as they saw fit. The Anglican Church was the official church of the colony, but when there were enough of another faith on hand to build a church of their own, no one interfered with them. This same principle applied to the many others who came to Virginia in her early years—Calvinists, Jews, Lutherans and freethinkers.

The Reverend Mr. Hunt conducted two services on Sunday mornings, and although attendance was not compulsory, Lord and Lady de la Warr attended regularly, so all other Anglicans went, too. By 1614–15, when the population rose to almost two thousand, a second Anglican church was built.

The state imposed two obligations on all of Jamestown's male residents, and no exceptions were granted. All men were members of the colony's militia, and were required to spend two or three hours every Sunday drilling, firing at targets with blunderbusses and loading and unloading the cannon in the fort. Every man, regardless of his vocation, was also required to spend *all* of his spare daylight time in growing crops for the entire community, joining fishing expeditions or going out into the forests on hunting and fowl-snaring expeditions. Until 1619 or thereabouts all food, including that which a man grew on property he claimed as his own, belonged to the community as a whole, and that which the farmer and his family had raised was returned to them in accordance with their own requirements. Although no one in Jamestown knew it, the colony was forced by nature, in its earliest days, to live according to a system that, two and a half centuries later, would be known as communism: every man produced according to his ability and received according to his needs.

By about 1619 the economy of the colony was sufficiently advanced to establish the system of private enterprise known in England. By then, too, Jamestown had seen its best days. Men began to realize the climate was not healthy, and were moving to other parts of Virginia to establish settlements. By the end of the nineteenth century erosion would make an island of the original colony's site, and seventy-five years later only a portion of the site would remain above water.

Originally decrees and laws were made and enforced by the President and Council, and later the Royal Governor ruled in the name of the Crown, making laws and relying on his military deputy to enforce them. Every male was obliged to carry firearms at all times, but anyone who fired at his neighbor was executed without benefit of a trial.

The basic laws of the colony were simple, and anyone who disobeyed them was placed on trial before the Governor or a deputy appointed by him. The decision of the judge was final in all cases, and appeals were unknown, there being no higher authority in the colony. A man who committed a theft was whipped, and the number of lashes he received depended on the extent of his crime. A man who stole a pair of moccasins from another might receive only ten lashes across his bare back, while he who stole food received one hundred lashes, and anyone who broke into the warehouses where food was stored was hanged after being whipped. No crime in Jamestown was as serious as that of stealing food.

Adultery and fornication with unmarried women was strictly forbidden. A man who committed a sex offense was whipped, then sent back to England, and a woman found guilty was returned to England on the first available ship. The poverty in England was so great that prostitution was common there, but there was none in Virginia, and Lord de la Warr was determined that there would be none. Between 1610 and 1615 five men and four women were deported from the colony on grounds of "immorality."

By 1610 Jamestown boasted a jail with two cells, a building of strong oak with double walls. Most of its inmates were confined there only for a day or two after committing breaches of the peace, usually becoming disorderly after drinking too much liquor.

The most vicious of crimes, in the opinion of the Crown and the Royal Governor, was treason, which included conspiracies of any kind against the administration. When committed by a commoner, such crimes were punishable by hanging, and when committed by an aristocrat, the punishment was beheading. There was no official executioner in the colony, and none was needed, there being no repetition of the many conspiracies that had disrupted the Council in the earliest days of the colony. Lord de la Warr held office on command of the King, and no one raised a hand against his authority.

Sir Thomas Dale commanded a military force of two officers, both lieutenants, and nineteen enlisted men. These troops, members of a regular Army Household regiment, had volunteered for duty in Virginia, and most eventually settled there. They assisted in the training of the militia, acted as a guard of honor for the Governor on ceremonial occasions, and when not otherwise occupied performed constabulary duties. Reports written by de la Warr and Dale indicate that the principal task of the soldiers was that of forcing shirkers to work in the fields, and occasionally they had to jail a man who became intoxicated.

The recreations of Jamestown were few, principally because there was so little spare time. The children engaged in foot races and played other games, but the men had virtually no opportunity to engage in sports. Lord de la Warr was an enlightened despot, one of the first rulers or viceroys anywhere who believed that one day all men would be literate, and he encouraged the colonists to learn to read and write. Education was compulsory for the children, an innovation unknown in England or on the Continent, which meant that within a few generations all who attended school would be literate. But there were many who moved to increasingly remote plantations in areas where no schooling was available, so another three hundred years would pass before literacy would become universal.

The literate spent at least some of their evenings reading, and other colonists paid calls on each other. No one was as yet earning any money, there were no coins in circulation, so there was no gambling, even though some of the colonists had been fond of card and dice games in England.

In the late spring of 1610, about a month after the arrival of the new administrators, Lord de la Warr and Sir Thomas Dale, escorted by Commodore Newport, paid a call on the Chickahominy. The new Governor deliberately traveled in style, his party filling several boats, and he took his military honor guard with him to impress the Indians.

In all, his party was made up of about forty persons, and to the astonishment of the Chickahominy a number of tents were raised on the banks of the river. De la Warr's own pavilion was made of silk, and Powhatan was so curious he inspected it himself. There could be little doubt in the mind of the Chief of Chiefs that the new ruler of Jamestown was a more important man than his predecessors. De la Warr and Sir Thomas wore plumed helmets of gleaming brass, their chainmail and corselets were silver and fine gems gleamed in the hilts of their dress swords. Their subordinates deferred to them with a display of obsequiousness that John Smith would have found amusing.

Whether Pocahontas took part in her tribe's entertainment of the distinguished English visitors is not known. Since she was no longer an inmate of the long house of the maidens she could have been present, at least to the extent of serving the guests their food as they sat around a cooking pit with Powhatan, Mataoko and the Bi-tan. Neither de la Warr nor Dale mentioned her in reports or correspondence, so they either did not meet her or they failed to remember her, the latter being unlikely.

In the autumn of 1610 Powhatan returned the Governor's visit and came to Jamestown for the first time, bringing with him a retinue of seventy or eighty of his people. Both of his sons joined him, as did his daughter, and the occasion marks Pocahontas's first authenticated appearance in the history of the English colony. She attended none of the discussions that her father and the elder of her brothers held with the Governor and his deputy, but she was very much in evidence throughout the visit of the Indians, which lasted for four or five days.

She created a sensation, and was the talk of Jamestown. Lord de la Warr mentioned her at length in his official reports, and Lady de la Warr wrote long letters about her to friends in London, as did Lady Dale, a lively and handsome young woman still in her twenties. For the first time in the life of Pocahontas it is possible to see and evaluate her through the eyes of Englishmen.

She was tall, Lady de la Warr wrote, with chiseled features and a natural grace and dignity that "endeared her to me." She was endowed with great feminine delicacy, but she demonstrated, too, that she could be as fiercely competitive as any young man. One afternoon during the Chickahominy visit, all normal activities in the colony having been suspended, a number of running and jumping contests were held, with young settlers and Chickahominy warriors in competition.

To the astonishment of the colonists Pocahontas was a participant in several foot races and gave a good account of herself. She won none of the contests, but crossed the finish line ahead of most of the Englishmen, and even managed to beat several young braves. But her participation did not detract from her femininity, and at all other times she was very much the young woman.

Her curiosity about English ways of life and manners was insatiable. She made a thorough inspection of the de la Warr and Dale homes, testing the beds, thoughtfully fingering a tapestry, staring for a long time at a portrait of Lady de la Warr and examining the many jars and bottles of cosmetics and unguents on the dressing table of her hostess. She was fascinated by the clothes of the English ladies and laughed incessantly as she was shown various undergarments and how to wear them.

Her first encounter with books seemed to puzzle her, and even when Lady Dale demonstrated their use, reading several paragraphs from a volume for her benefit, she appeared not to understand. Eventually she grasped the idea behind books, however, and thereafter, for the rest of her stay, she frequently picked up a book in the de la Warr or Dale homes, pointed to a word and demanded to know its pronunciation and meaning.

She was absorbed by what she saw in the kitchens of her hostesses, and spent the better part of a morning watching the Dale cook preparing dinner. Indoor fires and chimneys were new to her, and she seemed dazzled by the use of a number of pots and pans at the same time. She was stunned when she saw eggs cooking, was invited to make the experiment herself, and laughed when she tasted the results of her culinary efforts.

Perhaps the most poignant occasion on Pocahontas's initial visit to Jamestown was the party that Lady de la Warr gave in her honor while the men were negotiating a new trade agreement. A half-dozen English ladies of rank were present, and the only other Chickahominy was a girl slightly older than Pocahontas. It may be this was the girl Powhatan later took as his new wife. Neither Pocahontas nor the other Chickahominy understood a word of English, and the ladies were equally unfamiliar with the tongue of the Indians, so conversation had to be punctuated with the broad use of pantomime.

The significance of this little dinner can be appreciated only when it is remembered that everything Pocahontas saw and did was totally new to her. She sat down at a table for the first time; she had never before used a knife or fork, had no idea what to do with a napkin and had never seen glasses. She had never eaten an English meal, nor had she tasted either wine or tea.

Lady de la Warr and Lady Dale were acutely conscious of her situation, and both dwelt on the subject in their subsequent correspondence with relatives and friends in England. The other Indian girl was gauche, inept and obviously did not enjoy the experience. She ate little, made no attempts to participate in the conversation and fidgeted in her chair. But Pocahontas had the time of her life.

She was careful to observe all that her hostess did, and she behaved accordingly. She sat erect in her chair, looking regal and at the same time at ease. She flipped open her folded napkin and spread it across her lap as though she had been practicing the gesture. She raised her little finger in imitation of Lady de la Warr when she drank soup from a gourd, and after noting how to use a knife and fork she did the same, handling the dining implements as though she had used them all of her life.

She was quick to laugh at any minor errors she made, and insisted on performing various gestures a second and third time until she perfected them. She ate everything placed before her and enjoyed second helpings of some dishes. Unfortunately, neither Lady de la Warr nor Lady Dale discussed the menu of the meal in detail.

Only the wine was not to Pocahontas's liking. She made a wry face after taking only one sip, and then shuddered; she did not touch her glass again. But she drank tea with the verve and enthusiasm of a high-born Englishwoman. The beverage had been introduced to England only a few years earlier by the Dutch, and now was being imported in quantity for the first time by the newly formed East India Company, which would dominate the entire subcontinent of India before another century passed. English aristocrats had already demonstrated their liking for tea, and now that prices were being reduced the masses were taking to it, too. Pocahontas endeared herself to her hostess by sipping, draining her gourd and unabashedly asking for more.

On the last day of the Indians' visit to Jamestown the ladies presented Pocahontas with a gift of a complete English costume. She donned it in the presence of Lady de la Warr and Lady Warren, showing no reluctance to let them see her in the nude, and she admired her reflection at length in a pier-glass when she was dressed. She looked "like an enchantment," Lady de la Warr wrote, and seemed completely bemused. She found only the high-heeled shoes of the English aristocrat uncomfortable, and although she removed them after a few moments, she nevertheless refused to part with them.

The Indians had been given trinkets that were almost worthless since Jamestown had been founded, but Lady de la Warr now presented the Indian princess with a truly valuable gift, a chain and locket of gold, with a small diamond set in the locket. Pocahontas instantly appreciated the intrinsic worth of the jewelry, and although she had been taught from earliest childhood not to weep, tears came into her eyes as she fondled the locket. Lady de la Warr placed it around her neck and fastened it, and Pocahontas not only wore it for the rest of her life, but was buried with it still encircling her throat.

Other members of the Chickahominy party did not share Pocahontas's enjoyment of Jamestown. The colony had grown so large that Powhatan was more aware than ever of the threat the English posed to his own heretofore total domination of the area. And Mataoko made no secret of his dislike for his hosts. When the visitors were shown the cannon in the fort, the future ruler of the Chickahominy Confederation neither inspected the weapons nor appeared to be impressed when they were fired. He stood aside, his face impassive, registering neither awe nor fear.

Lord de la Warr rightly concluded that the Chickahominy crown prince would use his influence to turn his father against the colonists, and the Governor's feeling was confirmed when Pocahontas appeared before the other Indians in her English attire. Powhatan looked pleased and smiled at her, which was a natural reaction to the appearance of his favorite child. But Mataoko stared at his sister, his face stony and his eyes so dark they looked black. He said nothing to her in the presence of his English hosts, but Lord de la Warr wrote to the Privy Council that he would not be surprised to learn the silk gown Pocahontas was wearing was ripped from her body by her irate brother after they left the confines of Jamestown.

Apparently the reactions of Piaoko were not considered important. He had already visited the colony on a number of occasions, as has been seen, and his relations with the settlers had been amiable from the outset. Like his sister, he appreciated the comforts of the civilization the newcomers were bringing to America, and his love of hunting and fishing indicates that he liked to enjoy himself. He had fewer responsibilities than his brother, to be sure, so it is not surprising that he may have been less aware than Mataoko of the possibility that new waves of immigrants would restrict the influence of the Chickahominy. It is unlikely that any of the Indians could foresee the day when settlers from the British Isles would arrive in such vast numbers that the natives would be driven from their homes and hunting grounds. Had they known what was ahead, the Chickahominy, Tuscarora and other nations would have forgotten their grievances against each other and banded together to drive the invaders from their soil.

Certainly Pocahontas did not share the angry forebodings of Mataoko. What her brother may have said to her about the English is unknown, but the fifteen-year-old girl had a mind of her own, and if he attacked the settlers verbally, she paid no attention to him. After one visit to Jamestown Pocahontas had caught a glimpse of a world other than her own, and fell in love with it at first sight.

XII

On the surface the relations of the English and the Chickahominy remained amicable through the winter of 1610–11, and the usual amenities were observed. But Percy, Newport and others who had been dealing with the Indians for a number of years became apprehensive, and Lord de la Warr duly recorded their opinion to the effect that the friendship was cooling. When official parties of settlers went up the James River to obtain grain and furs and to bring the Indians axes, kegs of nails and other items arranged in the barter agreement, they found the atmosphere changed.

On previous occasions the English visitors had been

entertained at feasts, but now the Indians quietly gave them ordinary fare and went to no great effort on their behalf. Previously Powhatan had always received his guests in person and had shown them every courtesy, but now he did not see the English delegations. Neither Mataoko nor the Bi-tan were in evidence, either, and Percy, who accompanied one of the expeditions, later wrote that, for the first time, he felt the Chickahominy were displaying overt if controlled hostility.

How Pocahontas reacted to this changed atmosphere is unknown; in fact, no details of her life during the winter of 1610–11 are available. She herself never mentioned that period, so it is possible that her own relations with her father and elder brother were strained. Her brief visit to Jamestown had made her a confirmed Anglophile, while Powhatan and Mataoko were becoming worried by the rapid growth of the English colony.

In the early spring of 1611 Pocahontas made her second appearance in Jamestown, accompanying Piaoko and a party of braves who were delivering parched corn and furs to the colony under the terms of the most recent barter agreement. This visit was informal, but Lord and Lady de la Warr again went out of their way to treat the Indian princess with every consideration. She dined at the Governor's "mansion," and the Baron and his lady were delighted when she dressed in her English costume for the occasion.

By now she could speak a few words of English, and as she had learned them from Lady de la Warr, her accent was that of the aristocracy. The Chickahominy party happened to be in Jamestown on a Sunday, so Pocahontas accompanied the Governor and his lady to church. Her presence there caused a stir, and the Reverend Mr. Hunt delivered an extemporaneous sermon on the need for missionary work, which the colonists had neglected in their attempts to achieve their other objectives.

It has been said that this single visit to the Anglican church in Jamestown so inspired Pocahontas that she made up her mind to become a Christian. This story is a romanticized oversimplification of fact, and cannot be taken at face value. In view of all that happened in the years that followed, it is probable that the worship services left a favorable impression on Pocahontas, but it must be remembered that she spoke and understood virtually no English, so the celebration of the Eucharist must have been as incomprehensible to her as the sermon. Perhaps the singing of hymns by the entire congregation left a mark on her, and when she saw the colonists drop to their knees and pray, she must have realized that the church was a place dedicated to the adoration of a deity.

The girl spent her sojourn in Jamestown as the house guest of Lord and Lady de la Warr, and her hostess wrote an amused letter to her in-laws, the West family, about the experience. Never having slept in a "real" bed, Pocahontas did not trust the four-poster she found in her room, and spent the first night of her stay on the floor. The next day she laughed at herself, however, and obviously was determined to try something new, so thereafter she used the bed.

But she regarded the washbasins used by the settlers to cleanse themselves as absurd. At first she thought the basin and pitcher of water brought to her room were for purposes of drinking. She was disabused of the notion, and when she was shown how to use the basin, she laughed heartily. Then she raced down to the waterfront, stripped off her clothes and enjoyed a swim. The scandalized but nevertheless amused Lady de la Warr followed her to the bank of the river, waited for her to emerge onto the shore and then hastily wrapped her in a voluminous robe.

The experience taught Pocahontas a lesson, and no matter what her private opinion of English modesty may have been, she never again violated the taboos of the foreigners. For the rest of her stay she used her washbasin, even though the very idea may have been distasteful to her.

The contrast between her reaction to the customs and mores of her hosts and that of Piaoko and his braves was marked. When in Jamestown, the Indian princess lived as the English did. She ate all of her meals demurely seated at a table, never cross-legged in front of an open fire. She might watch the men of the town fishing, but did not participate, even though she was more expert than they. She refused ale and wine, for which the warriors showed a liking, and she always wore her English gown. Before she departed for the main town of the Chickahominy Lady de la Warr presented her with another gown. In return Pocahontas gave her hostess a small figure of stone that looked something like a bear, and this object became a treasured possession of the West family. Years later, after Pocahontas had mastered English, she revealed that the figure was her own handiwork.

According to a story that has persisted for more than three hundred and fifty years, Captain Samuel Argall, the ship's master who had brought the news to John Smith that a new government was being formed for the colony, saw Pocahontas during this sojourn in Jamestown, wanted her for himself and began to hatch a plot that would make her his. The tale is dramatic, but has no basis in fact, and what actually happened was sufficiently dramatic for any storyteller.

After a stay of a few days in the settlement, Pocahontas accompanied Piaoko and the braves back to the land of the Chickahominy. A short time later a message was received from Powhatan: the Chief of Chiefs demanded a large number of English fire sticks, bullets and gunpowder, and said he would break off trade relations unless he received them. It was obvious to de la Warr, West and the other officials of the colony that Powhatan wanted the weapons only for the purpose of driving the English settlers into the sea, so the demand was rejected.

Powhatan kept his word, abruptly terminating the barter agreement with the colony. Soon thereafter a small party of Chickahominy braves was seen in the neighborhood of Jamestown, but when they were hailed by some settlers, they made no response, and instead vanished into the forest.

The future appeared ominous, and Lord de la Warr summoned all of the men of the colony to a meeting. At that session a number of gentlemen-adventurers, strongly supported by a vocal element of the artisans, insisted that Piaoko and Pocahontas had known of the impending break and had come to Jamestown solely for purposes of spying on the settlement.

Lord de la Warr thought it absurd that Pocahontas should be regarded as a Chickahominy espionage agent, and Sir Thomas Dale agreed. The two leaders of the colony were willing to grant that they had no real understanding of the Indian mind, but it was inconceivable to them that the gentle, merry Pocahontas could be a party to a sinister plot. She was a lady, Dale said, and that ended the matter.

But the threat of war was serious, and the colony immediately strengthened its defense posture. Those who worked in the fields were forbidden to go alone beyond the Jamestown palisades, and were required to work in groups of three or four, always with their fowling pieces nearby. The system instituted by Captain John Smith was reinstated, and sentries were posted at the town gates and in the fort's watchtower around the clock.

No one knew whether or when actual hostilities might break out, and de la Warr was reluctant to send an emissary to the land of the Chickahominy, correctly feeling that the Indians would regard such action as an admission of weakness. It was at this juncture, in the middle of the summer of 1611, that Captain Samuel Argall stepped into the picture.

Argall was a typical product of his age, a hard-bitten, self-made master mariner who had known no compassion and felt none. Whether he had been present in Jamestown during Pocahontas's last visit a few weeks earlier or whether he had arrived since that time in his ship is irrelevant. He had his own ideas on how war could be averted, but he confided them to no one.

Instead he went to Lord de la Warr with a bold plan. The colonists were jittery because they didn't know the intentions of the Chickahominy, and he realized it was not feasible to send an ambassador to Powhatan. But the intrepid Argall proposed that he go to the main town of the Chickahominy on his own initiative, seemingly representing no one but himself. He had several old blunderbusses and pistols from which the hammers had been removed, rendering them useless, but he would offer them to the Chickahominy in trade, promising to return at a later date with ammunition and powder. The Indians would be eager to accept the bargain, and Argall, while in their town, would carefully observe whether the Chickahominy were preparing for war.

Lord de la Warr and his immediate subordinates were impressed, but pointed out to Argall that he was taking a great risk. If the Indians didn't believe his story and thought him a spy, they would take him into custody and possibly would torture and kill him. Argall insisted the possibility was slight, and received permission to make the effort.

Accompanied by his mate and a "small number" of his crew, probably three or four sailors, he traveled slowly up the James River, sailing in a shallop slightly larger than that which Newport and Smith had devised and used. The men deliberately took their time, hoping and believing that Chickahominy sentry outposts would take notice of their approach. After a journey of two days they reached the town of the Chickahominy shortly before sundown, and were coldly but correctly received by a small group of senior warriors and elders. Powhatan, his sons and the Bi-tan were conspicuous by their absence.

Argall, who had little or no familiarity with the language of the Chickahominy, made his offer, using pantomime freely. Then, as the Indians were about to withdraw in order to consider his offer, Argall indicated that he brought a personal message to Pocahontas from Lady de la Warr. One of the braves went to fetch the girl, and the others vanished, taking the guns with them.

It was Argall's hope that the Chickahominy would examine the blunderbusses at length, and, being unfamiliar with firearms, would not realize they were useless. Soon after the warriors departed with the weapons—while Argall waited on the otherwise deserted bank of the river—Pocahontas appeared in response to his summons. Argall did not wait for the men of the Chickahominy to end their deliberations.

A gag was placed over Pocahontas's mouth, her ankles and wrists were bound, and she was hidden beneath a pile of blankets carried in the shallop for that purpose.

The little party traveled downstream by night, ordinarily regarded as too dangerous, and made record time on their return journey to Jamestown. Pocahontas was kept hidden on the entire trip, Argall being afraid that unseen Chickahominy sentries might become aware of her abduction. Jamestown was reached late the following day after an uninterrupted journey of almost twenty-four hours.

Lord de la Warr and Sir Thomas Dale were horrified

118

when they learned what Argall had done, and the wildly indignant Pocahontas, after being released from her bonds, was taken off by Lady de la Warr, who tried to mollify her.

The Governor, his deputy and the other high officials of Jamestown felt certain the kidnapping would release the wrath of Powhatan, making war inevitable. But Argall demurred, boldly insisting his act would guarantee peace, as Powhatan would not make war while his beloved daughter remained a prisoner in the settlement.

All of the gentlemen-adventurers were summoned to a council, and the meeting lasted all night. Meanwhile Lady de la Warr gave Pocahontas clothes and a meal and tried to soothe the girl's ruffled feelings. She managed to convince the Indian princess that Lord de la Warr had known nothing of the kidnapping in advance. The girl's sense of humor was restored, and eventually she went to sleep in a guest bedchamber, wearing an ankle-length nightdress that belonged to her hostess.

Captain Argall was placed under arrest before the night ended, and was taken off to the Jamestown jail. The officials of the colony were so angry that, had war broken out as a result of the kidnapping, it is probable he would have been put to death.

By dawn the gentlemen-adventurers had hammered out a rough plan, the best they could conceive under the circumstances. Commodore Newport, whom the Chickahominy had regarded as a friend and who had a better understanding of the Indian language than anyone else in Jamestown, would leave at once for the main town of the Chickahominy. He would explain that the kidnapping had been plotted by one man without official cognizance, would present the Chief of Chief with gifts and promise him that Pocahontas would be returned unharmed in the immediate future.

Newport left at daybreak, several of his friends believing they would never see him again. Meanwhile Pocahontas slept at the house of the Governor and his lady. There she remained as an honored guest for the better part of a week, and when Newport returned, deeply perturbed, he insisted on telling his story in her presence.

Powhatan, he said, had been reluctant to see him, but finally had agreed to a meeting. He had accepted the various gifts that Newport gave him on behalf of the colony, and then he had listened stonefaced to the account of his daughter's abduction. He had made no comment on the subject, and had not indicated his own future intentions.

Pocahontas listened carefully to the story, with Newport repeating it to her as best he could in her own tongue, and she was not in the least surprised. She offered an explanation, which Newport then translated into English:

When an unmarried woman of the Chickahominy was captured—in war or otherwise—by the braves of another nation, she lost her standing as a Chickahominy and was regarded as the property of the nation that had taken her prisoner. Therefore, no matter how much Powhatan might grieve in private, he was forced to disown her. What became of her was not his concern or that of his people.

But, Pocahontas declared, he would not make war now on the English. Even if he had been preparing for hostilities against the colony, and she was unaware of what his intentions had been, he would lose face within and without the ranks of the Confederation if he attacked now. Other Indians would believe he was trying to avenge the kidnapping of his daughter, no matter what he might say to the contrary.

Lord de la Warr and the other officials were relieved to learn that the Chickahominy would not go to war against Jamestown, and Captain Argall was released from the jail, but was ordered to leave the colony without delay and never return.

Argall went back to England, indignant over the treatment he had received. He submitted a complaint in writing to the directors of the London Company, but they had no idea what to make of his tale, and therefore ignored it. At that point Argall disappeared from history, and nothing is known about the rest of his life.

Jamestown could not solve the problem of Pocahontas's presence as easily. She was free to leave whenever she wished, but it would be on the collective conscience of the settlers if she starved to death or was enslaved by the warriors of an independent nation not affiliated with the Chickahominy Confederation. Obviously the daughter of the Chief of Chiefs would be regarded as a great prize, regardless of the fact that custom had forced her father to disown her. And although Pocahontas knew the forest, it was easy to imagine that a slender girl of sixteen summers, thrown on her own resources, might starve or be attacked by wild beasts.

There was only one possible solution, and Lord de la Warr undoubtedly spoke for his immediate subordinates, the gentlemen-adventurers and the commoners of Jamestown when he invited Pocahontas to make her permanent home in the colony.

She agreed, and appeared supremely happy. But her presence caused a variety of new problems for which there were no precedents. There were too many woman-hungry bachelors in the settlement for a lovely girl unfamiliar with English mores to live alone and unattended. She didn't understand the language, and she would have to learn English customs and manners. The Governor and his lady could not take her permanently into their own home because their official duties kept them too busy. So what could be done with the Indian princess?

Sir Thomas Dale and his wife resolved the dilemma by offering Pocahontas a home with them. Arabella, Lady Dale, who was related to the West family, was a handsome, brilliant young woman who had been mistrusted by her peers in England, who considered her too wise for her own good. A seventeenth-century lady was not expected to be endowed with an intellect of her own. Lady Dale was still childless, and as she and her husband employed two servants, she had little to occupy her time. Sir Thomas was one of the busiest men in Jamestown, so his wife may have welcomed the diversion that was offered her.

Had Pocahontas been given a choice in the matter she might have preferred to remain in the home of Governor. Lady de la Warr had become and was to remain her special friend and confidante for the rest of her life. But she had no cause for complaint: the Dales were charming, Arabella was regarded as the most beautiful woman in the colony, and Sir

Thomas was a man of high estate in England as well as in Jamestown. A new wing, consisting of a bedchamber and a small sitting room, was built onto the one-story Dale house, and in the late summer of 1611 Pocahontas moved into her own quarters and began a new phase of her extraordinary life.

XIII

Guesswork about the life of Pocahontas ends with her removal to Jamestown in the summer of 1611. Everything she did and everything of consequence that happened to her thereafter was documented, and all that remains unknown are her feelings and reactions to the overwhelming changes that took place in her way of life.

Jamestown, to be sure, was a way station, a halfway point between the civilization of the Chickahominy and that of people who lived in England. The colonists brought the customs, mores and morals of the Old World with them to the New, but, as has already been seen, they themselves were changed by the wilderness in which they settled, and they adopted many of the habits of the Indians.

One of the first of the many tasks that confronted Pocahontas was that of learning a new language. The Reverend Mr. Hunt volunteered to become her instructor, and no one in the colony better suited the assignment. He was dedicated to his profession, had no interest in her as a woman and possessed the zeal of the true missionary. Fate or coincidence intervened, too. In the early summer of 1611 a group of more than fifty distinguished English scholars completed the task of making a new translation of the Holy Bible which had been commissioned by King James in 1604. The new version, which retained many features of older versions but was rich in language and simile, was published in 1611, and a number of copies were sent to the distant colony in the New World. The King James Bible, as it was known from the time of its publication, was printed in large folios and sold for thirty shillings, a relatively modest price that brought it within reach of the middle class and contributed materially to the spread of literacy in the British Isles.

The copies that came to Newport were placed in the keeping of the Reverend Mr. Hunt, who was not only fascinated by the work himself, but would have been remiss in his duties had he not used the Bible as Pocahontas's textbook when he taught her English. She read no other book, and although she conversed daily with the Dales and others, her study of English was concentrated, in the main, on the Bible. She proved to be a remarkably apt pupil, and made such rapid progress that, by Christmas of 1611, a scant five months after she began to make her home in Jamestown, she was able to recite long passages from the Books of Genesis, Psalms and Matthew from memory.

The Anglicization of the Indian princess was complete, and she turned wholeheartedly to the ways of her new people, but in the process she adapted many of their habits to her old ways. The indoor, wood-burning stoves of Jamestown were clumsy, downdrafts often sent fumes spewing into living quarters, and the women of the colony considered their kitchens a menace. Pocahontas solved the problem by utilizing the cooking methods of the Chickahominy, and an adaptation of her kitchen became standard throughout England's North American colonies in the next one hundred and fifty years. She separated the kitchen from the main portion of the house, building an extension that was sometimes connected with the main portion of the dwelling by a covered or semicovered passage. In the kitchen she dug a pit, lined it with stones, then placed a chimney or air vent directly over it.

In the early days of the colonies many kitchens followed her system without change, but most Caucasian women were accustomed to actual stoves rather than cooking pits, and built up their ranges accordingly. In the main, however, Pocahontas's use of a separate building was followed, and the chimney or air vent was placed directly over the stove, just as she placed it over the pit she constructed in an outbuilding behind the house of Sir Thomas and Lady Dale.

Featherbeds were considered a necessity in England, and were used by all classes, but domesticated fowl were scarce in the New World and feathers difficult to obtain. Again Pocahontas solved the problem in her own way, thanks to her Chickahominy background. The first time she slept in a featherbed she found it too soft for her comfort, so she "invented" a new kind of mattress that was a cross between the English and the Chickahominy versions. She sewed cloth around a pallet of tender pine boughs, which prevented the pine needles from pricking the flesh of a sleeper. This bed was inexpensive, easily disposable when it became dirty and, above all, comfortable for those who did not want to sink far into the depths of a mattress when they went to sleep.

Within a few years most Jamestown settlers were sleeping on the mattress Pocahontas developed; thereafter the custom spread to other colonies and ultimately to Kentucky and Tennessee when the lands west of the mountains were opened to colonization. Featherbeds were used by the aristocrats and the middle-class merchants in major American cities, of course, but were spurned on the frontier, largely because they were impractical. Most who slept on cloth-covered pine boughs had no idea they were in the debt of Pocahontas.

The Indian princess made a contribution to the eating

habits of the colonists, too. Rare and exotic foods were difficult to obtain in a land where the threat of starvation was ever-present when every new colony was founded. And the settlers were so busy making homes for themselves in the wilderness and planting crops that they had no time for "fancy cooking." But the nobles came from a land where as many as a dozen courses were served each day at dinner, and the middle class liked to emulate those above them.

Futile attempts were made in Jamestown, after women began to arrive there in significant numbers in 1610, to prepare more elaborate meals than the earliest settlers in the all-male community had known. The failures came to a halt only a year later, when Pocahontas began to make her presence in the colony felt. She showed the women a number of ways to use cornmeal in various dishes, and her utilization of wild fruits and root vegetables was ingenious. Above all, she taught the good ladies of Jamestown that no meats were more succulent than those that were roasted over an open fire and basted in their own fat.

Arabella Dale wrote to friends in London that, on a number of occasions, Pocahontas insisted on preparing the main meal of the day, and the meats she cooked were unique. Other women began to use the Indian princess' simple Chickahominy recipes, which the women of the tribe had handed down from mother to daughter for generations, and the colony formed eating habits that eventually became standard throughout Virginia, then spread to other colonies.

Only in matters of dress and grooming did Pocahontas become the slave of English fashion, perhaps because the dress of the Chickahominy was unattractive and lacked femininity. The Indian girl happily adopted the customs of the ladies around her, and did not complain as she donned many layers of complicated undergarments, thick stockings and, when necessary, girdles that further diminished the size of her already tiny waist.

The styles of the early seventeenth century were perfect for a young woman who was tall, exceptionally slender and had an erect bearing. She could wear a low-cut gown or a large, ruffled stock with a flair that was her own, and she learned to handle long skirts with grace. The shoes of English women caused her problems for at least a year or two, but she got used to them, and after 1613 or 1614 never again was seen barefooted, either in public or in her own home.

At no time did Pocahontas wear veils, however, or conceal her face behind a fan. And her hairstyles changed with the time of day. Jamestown became accustomed to the sight of her waist-long hair hanging freely down her back, a style that did not become popular for another three and a half centuries and for which no credit can be given to Pocahontas. But she presented a dramatically altered appearance on social occasions, when, presumably with the initial assistance of Lady Dale and Lady de la Warr, she wore her hair piled high on her head in a variety of styles. She became adept in the use of combs, and one of her favorites was an ornately carved Spanish comb of white ivory that her husband presented to her as a gift.

The women of Jamestown knew better than to compete with Pocahontas, whose beauty was unique. Lady Dale, whose portraits reveal that she was blonde and fair-skinned, enjoyed appearing at the side of her guest because of the sharp, pleasant contrast in appearance they offered together.

The position of Pocahontas in the Dale household was somewhat similar to that of a younger sister, a ward or a niece. She enjoyed the protection of Sir Thomas, whose duties had been expanded to those of a deputy Governor, and the men of the colony knew they would be held responsible for any untoward incidents. But Pocahontas was free to come and go as she pleased, and neither of the Dales tried to restrict her movements. Just as her presence in Jamestown was voluntary, she placed herself under the authority of her hosts.

Her permanent presence in the community excited general, continuing interest, and at no time did anyone take her for granted, but the bachelors kept their distance. Sir Thomas made it clear by his attitude that he would be displeased if anyone made advances to his charge, and his stature was so great that no one dared to cross him.

During Pocahontas's first year in Jamestown she appears to have concentrated the better part of her time and attention on learning English. She spent an hour or two each day with the Reverend Mr. Hunt, and she studied the King James Bible incessantly. As she mastered words and sentences she became increasingly interested in the ideas she was reading, and began to question the clergyman about the content of the Bible.

It was then that her real religious education was inaugurated. It appears to have been unnecessary to wean her away from the pantheistic, nature-worshipping faith of her ancestors, which seems to have become less influential as she became increasingly engrossed in Christian theology. Certainly the Reverend Mr. Hunt knew her conversion would be regarded as a triumph by the Church of England bishops and by King James, the titular head of the Church. In an age when royalty was all powerful, when kings ruled by Divine Right and the authority of monarchy as an institution was everywhere regarded as absolute, the conversion of the daughter of a ruler would be a stunning victory. One of King James's titles was Defender of the Faith, and in his eyes as well as those of his subjects, Pocahontas's acceptance of Anglican Christianity would justify the effort, expense and sacrifice that had been necessary to establish a colony in the New World.

The first mention of Pocahontas's approaching conversion appears not in the reports or correspondence of Lord de la Warr or his deputy, but in a sermon delivered in Westminster Abbey in the presence of the King, Queen and Prince Charles, who succeeded to the title of Prince of Wales when his brother Henry died. The revelation was made by the actual head of the Church, the Reverend George Abbot, Archbishop of Canterbury, who "rejoiced in the goodness of the Almighty, who has opened the eyes of a heathen princess and shown her the True Light of Faith." Apparently the Reverend Mr. Hunt had written to his superiors to tell them that Pocahontas was about to become a Christian, but his letter has not survived the passage of time.

The Archbishop revealed the news in January, 1613, and in March of that year Pocahontas actually became a member of the Anglican Church. She was baptized, confirmed and took Holy Communion in a special service which Lord de la Warr described in a detailed report to the Crown.

All of Jamestown's officials were present, and the ladies and gentlemen of the community sat in the front pews. Every seat in the church, which held about one hundred and fifty persons, was occupied, and a "great crowd" spilled out into the yard, the doors remaining open so all could hear what transpired inside. Pocahontas was dressed in a gown of white silk made for the occasion by a woman who had been a seamstress in London before coming to the New World, and a choir of forty "raised their voices in thanksgiving to God."

When the service ended, the cannon in the fort boomed a salute, and the people cheered as Pocahontas left the church on the arm of the Governor. A holiday had been declared for the occasion, and everyone repaired to Smith Field, where roasted meats, barley cakes and wine were served. The weather was still chilly, but no one minded, and Pocahontas was radiant. By now she had gained command of the English language and was able to chat easily and volubly with the throngs who approached to congratulate her.

Like so many converts from one faith to another throughout history, Pocahontas took Christianity seriously, and no one in Jamestown was more devout. She attended church regularly, and frequently stayed for the second Sunday service after offering her prayers at the first. There was "no woman more holy in all of Christendom," Lord de la Warr was pleased to inform the Crown.

A special service of thanksgiving was held in Westminster Abbey in July, 1613, with Archbishop Abbot conducting. It was attended by King James, Queen Anne and their respective suites, and the entire Privy Council turned out, as did many of the other leading nobles. If Captain John Smith was in London at the time he must have known of the service, but if he attended it, that fact was not recorded, since he was not of sufficient importance to be noted.

In any event, Pocahontas was a celebrity in England long before she came to London. In Jamestown she was universally regarded as a member of the ruling hierarchy, and spent virtually all of her time with the gentry. Social distinctions were marked in the seventeeth century; classes did not mix and the lower orders did not try to rise above their station. But America was already breaking down class barriers and creating a breed different from any that was known in the British Isles or on the Continent. Noble and commoner who daily faced the hazards of wilderness living together found it natural to fraternize, and although they would not have dined at the same table in the Old World, they did so in the New without strain or self-consciousness. A man's life depended on the good will and cooperation of his neighbor, and danger knew no class distinctions.

So men who would have remained in the back hall of Sir Thomas Dale's London house were free to sit in the "grand parlor" of his simple Jamestown home. But they came only at his invitation, the process of removing class lines having just been initiated. The people Pocahontas saw most frequently were Lord and Lady de la Warr and Sir George and Lady Somers. It was natural for her to have formed her friendships in the highest of Jamestown circles since, as a child, she had stood apart from other Chickahominy children.

Other factors entered into the picture, too. Class distinctions in the seventeenth century, as in so many other periods, were noted by speech patterns and manners, and Pocahontas was taught by aristocrats, so she spoke and behaved like a lady. Only Captain Argall had treated her in an undignified manner, and now, when she walked down the dirt roads of Jamestown, the artisans touched their stocking caps as she passed. In all probability she took their respect for granted.

The education of the Indian princess continued and broadened as her stay in Jamestown grew longer, and it is staggering to realize how much she had to learn. She knew nothing of history, government, politics, science or the arts, her horizon having been limited by the circumscribed world of the Chickahominy. Now she was thrown into the company of a group of the most sophisticated and best educated of English aristocrats, and only by reading could she begin to catch up with them.

Lady de la Warr wrote that Pocahontas frequently borrowed books from the Governor's library, and the Reverend Mr. Hunt often came to the Dale house with other books for her, which he selected himself. Her reading was eclectic and she appears to have been interested in all subjects, but in time she began to specialize. The theater fascinated her, but it is not known whether she read any of the plays written and produced during England's golden age of the theater. The works of Shakespeare, Ben Jonson, Beaumont, Fletcher and a dozen others were filling London theaters, but there were no theaters in the struggling New World colony. Perhaps Pocahontas obtained folio copies of some of the more popular plays of the period and read them.

She also developed a great interest in medicine, at that time a blend of science and superstition. There were two physicians in Jamestown, as well as a surgeon-barber, and according to Sir Thomas Dale, she discussed prescriptions with them as well as the cures for various ailments.

In 1613 Pocahontas was eighteen years of age, a woman by the standards of the English and well into maturity according to the mores of the Chickahominy. Until now, however, she had demonstrated no interest in the opposite sex, but that would soon be rectified.

XIV

By 1613 there may have been as many as two hundred to two hundred and fifty women in the Jamestown settlement, but they were still overwhelmingly outnumbered by the men, so any single girl was the center of the eligible bachelors' attention. Earlier in Pocahontas's stay in the colony she must have attracted the interest of men, but the attitude of Sir Thomas Dale kept them at arm's length. Eventually, however, it became impossible to isolate her any longer, and Sir Thomas let it be known that he would not discourage suitors for her hand. Whether he himself was responsible for this decision or whether Arabella dropped a word to him in response to a hint from Pocahontas is not known. A lady living in the early seventeenth century was not considered forward if she welcomed the attentions of gentlemen.

The Dale house, as an amused and pleased Lady de la Warr wrote to members of the West family in London, soon resembled a honeypot to which countless flies were drawn. Every bachelor of the gentleman-adventurer set began to pay formal calls on Pocahontas, and the experience must have been as difficult for her as it was a bore for Lady Dale, who was forced by the requirements of society to act as her chaperone. Specific rules had to be rigidly observed, and nothing in the past life of the Indian princess had prepared her for such an ordeal.

A gentleman was expected to call on a lady between four and five o'clock in the afternoon, but the hour was wrong for Jamestown, where everyone worked in the fields until sundown. When the men returned to town from their labors, they were hungry, and since Sir Thomas could not be expected to entertain dinner guests every night of the week, the visits had to be postponed. It was finally agreed that those who wished to pay court to Pocahontas would call between eight and nine o'clock in the evening.

The supply of candles in the Dale house diminished rapidly. Pocahontas sat on one side of the parlor, her caller perched on a hard chair or bench opposite her, and Lady Dale, who participated in the conversation to whatever extent pleased her, occupied middle ground. Under no circumstances was a gentleman permitted to discuss personal matters, but there was no royal court in Jamestown to gossip about, no theatrical performance to be dissected, no political dispute to be rehashed and relished. And any talk about the colonial administration was out of bounds, too; the gentlemen-adventurers could not allow themselves to forget that their hostess was the wife of the deputy Governor, a man who had acquired a reputation as a stern taskmaster.

This left a limited number of topics, which Arabella Dale listed in a letter to a friend in England:

1. The sermon last delivered by the Reverend Mr. Hunt.

2. The next sermon he would deliver.

3. The potential size of the current corn crop.

4. The quality of the beans and peas being grown in communal gardens.

5. The inexplicable disappearance of mackerel and bluefish from the salt waters in the vicinity of the colony, which was balanced by the unexpected appearance of a flat fish with white meat, weighing between five and seven pounds, currently being caught in large numbers.

6. Chickahominy methods of food storage.

7. The Chickahominy religion.

8. Hunting prospects on the upper reaches of the James River, in the vicinity of the falls.

For night after night these same subjects were hauled out, polished and discarded. But Pocahontas smiled, nodded and encouraged the shy and the clumsy. No refreshments other than tea were offered; sack would have been customary, too, had the suitors called in London, but spirits were difficult to obtain in the New World, and Sir Thomas guarded his supply.

A caller ordinarily was permitted to make three visits, each time leaving his gloves on a small table located in the front hall. If the lady handed him his gloves at the end of this third visit, she was letting him know that he could call again. If she allowed him to pick up the gloves himself, however, his visits were terminated. The first and only suitor whose gloves Pocahontas picked up was Samuel Dooling, a young gentleman-adventurer with imposing family connections. He was the youngest son of a viscount who held a post at Whitehall, and his uncle was a prominent Anglican bishop reportedly first in line for the vacant archbishopric of York, the second highest ecclesiastical post in the Anglican Church.

Lord de la Warr and Sir Thomas Dale heartily approved of Dooling as a prospective husband for Pocahontas. Jamestown had become self-sufficient to the extent that communal farming was being abandoned, and individual gentlemen-adventurers were acquiring and farming their own properties. Dooling had taken possession of a large farm the previous year, hired a number of men to work with him and was showing promise of succeeding in the enterprise. His father's prominence at court made it distinctly possible that he would be given a knighthood after he became Pocahontas's consort, and Lord de la Warr, in a letter to his fellow directors of the London Company, suggested that discreet inquiries be made on the matter at Whitehall.

Competition having been eliminated, Dooling was Pocahontas's only suitor in the autumn of 1613. They were not yet formally betrothed but everyone expected that, in due time, Sir Thomas and Lady Dale would announce their engagement. Before the end of the year, however, Dooling suddenly sold his farm property to another gentleman-adventurer and left the New World, never to return. Presumably he was in England when Pocahontas went there a few years later, but he appears to have absented himself from the many receptions, assemblies and other functions given in her honor.

The cause of the abrupt termination of the romance is unknown. According to later sources, Pocahontas developed an interest in the man she married, but he did not arrive in Jamestown until a month or two after Dooling's departure. It must suffice that the lady exercised her feminine prerogative and changed her mind.

John Rolfe had been a member of the expedition that had set out for Jamestown in 1610, but he had remained in Bermuda after being forced to spend a winter there. A widower, he came to Jamestown with his two small children, John and Barbara, arriving in January or February, 1614, although some authorities believe he arrived several years earlier.

A portrait of him made in later years reveals him as an exceptionally tall, dignified man with a lean face and high forehead, a direct gaze and firm mouth. He had the dark eyes, hair and coloring of a Cornishman, wore a small beard and, like most Englishmen who spent considerable time in the New World, scorned the use of a wig. Rolfe was about ten years older than Pocahontas.

Having inherited valuable farmlands from his father, Rolfe was one of the wealthier settlers, but unlike most of the other gentlemen who came to the New World, he was no adventurer, one of the few who was not taken in by the talk of the gold and precious gems to be found in America. Rolfe was a businessman who believed there was a fortune to be made in tilling the soil. What he had in mind specifically was tobacco, the "green gold" that England was beginning to import in ever-larger quantities. Few men anywhere were engaged in the systematic cultivation of tobacco, and it occurred to Rolfe that a fortune awaited the farmer who developed a strain that would be pleasing to both pipe smokers and snuff users. Furthermore, the tobacco produced by Spain's empire was exorbitantly expensive, out of reach of all but the wealthiest aristocrats, and success was certain for the man who would mass-produce tobacco for the English market.

Rolfe had experimented with a strain native to Bermuda, but had found it too delicate. However, he had brought a number of plants with him to Jamestown, and when he crossed the Bermuda strain with the coarser tobacco he found growing wild in Virginia, the result was a slow-burning, aromatic blend, which was hailed as the finest tobacco on earth. The English demand for it was insatiable, and the French, Dutch, Germans and Scandinavians wanted it, too. Even the Spaniards finally admitted it was superior to the tobacco they grew in South and Central America.

The industrious, sober Rolfe developed his new strain of tobacco during his first season in Jamestown, and found the Virginia soil and climate perfect. By the following year he had planted one hundred acres, and thereafter he sold plants to other settlers while continuing to expand his own holdings. Evenutally he and his heirs owned tobacco plantations covering more than twenty-five hundred acres, and he has come down in history as the father of the lucrative Virginia tobacco industry.

At first glance the differences in the ages and backgrounds of Pocahontas and John Rolfe make them appear to have been unlikely partners, and the presence of his two small children should have made a romance between them even more remote. But Rolfe, although worldly, was very devout, and it is probable that he and Pocahontas first met at the Jamestown church. There is no record of the early days of their relationship, but many years later their son said they had fallen in love at their initial meeting.

Pocahontas was now nineteen, a mature woman by the

standards of both the Chickahominy and the English, and Rolfe's children aroused her maternal instincts. Sir Thomas and Lady Dale readily agreed when she asked their permission to move little Barbara and John the younger in with her while their father built his new house. In this way the couple saw each other regularly, and by spring Lady de la Warr was already writing to relatives and friends in England that the Indian princess had a substantial, well-regarded suitor.

Rolfe, a graduate of Oxford University, was a student of languages, and Pocahontas taught him to speak the tongue of the Chickahominy. By the following year he became sufficiently adept to deal direct with Powhatan and other members of the Confederation, from whom he insisted on purchasing land rather than follow the usual early settlers' custom of seizing whatever property they wanted.

By the summer of 1614, Lady de la Warr reported to the West family, Rolfe's house in Jamestown was ready for occupancy, and was far larger than a widower with two small children ordinarily would need. It had two sitting rooms, a sewing room, a library and a lady's dressing room, a luxury that only Lady de la Warr and Lady Dale had enjoyed in the New World. So it was apparent to the most casual observer that Rolfe planned to be married in the near future.

There was no color barrier between Rolfe and Pocahontas, each accepting the other as an equal, and it was their adoption of this attitude that set a precedent tens of thousands of others would follow. The colonists who came to the New World took the property of the Indians, harassed and fought them, and in general behaved toward them in a cavalier manner that was not recognized until the twentieth century, but at no time did they regard the Indians as inferiors. Few attempts were made to enslave them, such efforts almost always ending in failure, and there were many successful intermarriages during the decades and centuries that followed.

Pocahontas and Rolfe were married in the Jamestown church on September 11, 1614, with the bride adopting the Old Testament name of Rebecca, the daughter-in-law of Abraham, the father of the Jewish people. The original Rebecca, found in Genesis 24 and 25, was the wife of Isaac and the mother of Esau and Jacob, and although there has been a great deal of speculation on the subject, posterity has no positive information regarding Pocahontas's reasons for adopting the name. Thereafter she was known interchangeably as the Princess Pocahontas and the Lady Rebecca, the latter being a courtesy title as Rolfe, although the younger son of an aristocrat, inherited no title of his own.

The bride was given away by Sir Thomas Dale, and wore the same white dress and veil in which she had appeared at her baptism and confirmation. Many authorities have claimed that the wedding ceremony was performed by the Rev. Richard Rusk. This contention is based on certain information which indicates that the Rev. Hunt had died in 1608 or 1609. The occasion was doubly significant because Powhatan, accompanied by a party of about forty, came to Jamestown to see his daughter married. Two elderly Indian women, to whom Pocahontas showed marked deference, were introduced as her aunts; posterity has never learned their names. Piaoko also attended, and thereafter was such a frequent visitor to the home of his sister and brother-in-law that Jamestown took his presence for granted and paid little attention to his comings and goings.

The Englishmen present happily followed their custom of kissing the bride, but the Chickahominy made no departures from their own traditions. Lady de la Warr, a shrewd and constant observer, noted that Pocahontas, exchanged no gestures of affection with her father and other relatives, and that there was no physical contact between them.

But Powhatan enjoyed himself sufficiently to stay for three days of festivities. This was his first visit to the colony since Lord de la Warr had become Governor, and the authorities took full advantage of the presence of the Chief of Chiefs. For the first time it was possible to hold full-scale discussions because Pocahontas acted as the interpreter for both sides, thereby enabling her father and the Governor to express their views fully in the knowledge that they would be accurately represented.

A number of discussions were held over a two-day period, and the results assured peace between the colonists and the Chickahominy Confederation. Trade relations were restored on a large-scale basis, and Lord de la Warr felt Jamestown was secure now, so he reversed Captain John Smith's policy of selling no arms to the Indians. Perhaps he agreed to trade blunderbusses, ammunition and gunpowder for furs because the fowling pieces were so notoriously inaccurate. Cannon and pistols, which were far deadlier weapons in the early seventeenth century, were not included in the deal.

The treaty was not reduced to writing because the Chickahominy had no written language, and this unfortunate fact led to innumerable and tragic misunderstandings in later years. A rough border was drawn between the two domains, with each promising not to poach on the preserves of the other. Baron de la Warr was scrupulous in his observance of the treaty, as was Sir Thomas Dale, who succeeded him as Governor and was present during the talks. But so many Englishmen, Scotsmen and Irishmen settled in Virginia in the decades to come that the pressure to obtain land was too great; eventually the borders of the Chickahominy were violated and their land seized.

It was of the greatest significance that Mataoko did not attend the wedding of Pocahontas, but at the time no one appears to have been unduly upset or alarmed by his absence. What Pocahontas herself may have felt in private about her brother's snub is unknown. Mataoko did not approve of the union of a Chickahominy princess with an Englishman, and showed his displeasure by staying at home.

It is surprising that the colonists failed to make any intensive attempts to win the friendship of the future Chief of Chiefs. Perhaps they were so relieved because they had established the best of terms with Powhatan that they failed to think of what might happen when his son succeeded him. That lack of foresight would be costly in the years ahead.

Whether Pocahontas herself realized that her brother's opposition would mean trouble in the future is impossible to determine. Certainly she had taken no part in the deliberations of her father's Council in her formative years, and women played no political role in Jamestown, either, so she may have been ignorant of the possible consequences.

More over, she was a bride of only a day when her father and Lord de la Warr initiated their talks, interrupting her honeymoon so she could act as an interpreter, and it is not too far-fetched to assume that her thoughts were centered on Rolfe, their life together and the rearing of her stepchildren, rather than on the problems Mataoko's absence might mean for Jamestown in the future. Even if she did recognize impending trouble, which is possible, there was nothing practical she could do about the situation. Only Powhatan had the authority to order his elder son to come to Jamestown for the wedding, and the Chief of Chiefs had elected not to exercise that prerogative.

It was enough for everyone present that Powhatan appeared and made his peace with the colony. For now, Jamestown could ask for no more, and the people regarded Pocahontas as a heroine and the symbol of their good fortune.

XV

Pocahontas once again demonstrated her remarkable, chameleonlike quality, her ability to cope with new ways of life and situations alien to her, when she became Mistress Rolfe. She appears to have adapted herself quite easily to her roles as colonial housewife, stepmother and ultimately as mother. Not only was she completely at home in the house Rolfe built for her, but she became an efficient manager, which could not have been easy in a raw, frontier community. She had two servants, both of them English colonists, one working as a cook and the other an all-around maid and part-time nursemaid.

According to an ancient saying, no man is a hero to his valet, and by the same token no lady is a heroine to her cook, but Pocahontas appears to have been the exception. The woman who worked for her was Elizabeth Reedy, a Londoner in her mid-twenties who had just arrived in Jamestown as an immigrant and who had worked in the kitchen of one of England's great households. Perhaps, after suffering the formality and discipline that prevailed in an aristocratic kitchen, where there may have been as many as a dozen persons on the staff, the woman enjoyed the friendly, easy life in a Jamestown household.

She later married a man named Dodge, and her son, Henry, who was proud of his mother's association with the Indian princess, wrote that Pocahontas, although never losing her dignity, treated her cook more as a colleague than as a servant. The mistress of the house frequently worked in the kitchen at her cook's side, simultaneously teaching her recipes and learning more herself about English cooking.

Pocahontas planted and tended her own vegetable garden behind the Rolfe house, a miniature farm of about an acre or two. After her own labors in the fields of the Chickahominy, the efforts she expended must have seemed like child's play. She grew beans, peas and onions, the vegetable staples of the colony, and apparently her crops were large enough for the needs of her own table. It has been claimed, without substantiation, that she was the first American to grow squash and potatoes. Enthusiasts have tried to portray Pocahontas as the paragon of all virtues and as an initiator beyond compare; her demonstrated record is impressive, but many claims have been unverifiable and should be regarded with skepticism.

Pocahontas made a happy, comfortable home for her husband, completely adapting to his way of life. She quickly acquired a reputation as a splendid hostess, and her friends— Lady de la Warr, Lady Dale and Lady Somers—had nothing but praise for her in their letters. They accepted her on their own level, not as an oddity, and their attitude toward her contained no hint of patronization.

The Rolfe children were entered in the classes in the

two-room Jamestown schoolhouse, but the basic education they received there was incomplete, and Pocahontas also taught them at home. Here was a young woman who, a few years earlier, had been a savage by the standards of England and the Continent. Now she was sufficiently advanced to teach reading, grammar, writing and arithmetic to her stepchildren. She herself was studying Greek and Latin under the tutelage of the Reverend Mr. Hunt, but was not yet proficient enough to pass along what she knew.

She took complete charge of the children's religious education, however, and her zeal was unflagging. Many years later, after Barbara Rolfe had married Sir Frederick Butler, a prominent supporter of the house of Stuart in Parliament, she wrote that her stepmother had discussed the Bible for at least an hour each day with her and her brother, had forced them to read extensively in both the Old and New Testaments, and had quizzed them at length on what they had studied. Attendance at worship services was obligatory in the Rolfe family, and Pocahontas accepted no excuse from a child who would have preferred to spend a Sunday morning playing.

In some respects Pocahontas modified the customs of the English aristocrats, who saw little of their children. Barbara and John the younger dined with their father and stepmother daily, generally eating the main meal of the day with them in the early afternoon. They were given their supper at a different time, however, and Pocahontas dined alone with her husband in the evening.

Until 1614 or 1615, candles provided the houses of Jamestown with their only illumination, but at about that time the first lamps came to the colony from England. Oil was scarce, however, and so expensive that even the wealthiest colonists were forced to use their lamps sparingly. But an enterprising settler discovered a method of refining the oil of cod and tuna, and this helped to relieved the shortage. Not until later in the century were various vegetable oils imported from the Caribbean islands for use in lamps.

The burning of a lamp was considered such a luxury that most people, including the Governor and Lady de la Warr, saved their oil for evenings when they entertained.

Pocahontas, always the individualist, preferred to light a lamp when she and Rolfe ate their evening meal. As a consequence, they entertained by candlelight.

Guests were invited frequently, and included many visitors other than the members of the Rolfe's immediate circle. John thought of himself as a "simple farmer," according to the later accounts of his children, and his door was open to every Jamestown resident. In addition, Pocahontas's popularity was so great that, at one time or another, virtually every member of the community called on her.

In spite of her beauty, the women of the colony were not jealous of Pocahontas, probably because she observed the middle-class proprieties, among them that of never flirting with married men, and because it was so obvious she was in love with her husband. Rolfe was always present in her conversations, and she never tired of praising his patience, wisdom and virtue.

In later life Rolfe was known to English contemporaries as a silent, withdrawn man, but it well may be the tragedies he had suffered by that time left permanent marks on his disposition. During the years of his marriage to Pocahontas he appears to have shared her appreciation of life. He developed a recreational interest in fishing, and whenever he caught a fish of a species unknown to him, she identified it for him by its Chickahominy designation. The name of the snapper, which is found in quantity off the coasts of the Southern states, is said to be a variation of Chickahominy nomenclature.

Pocahontas gave up her own active interest in sports after her marriage and became a sedate colonial matron. When Piaoko paid his frequent visits to Jamestown, she no longer hunted and fished with him, and Rolfe went in her stead. Such men's activities were not deemed appropriate for seventeenth-century ladies, so Pocahontas abandoned them, and occupied her time with gentler duties. She learned to spin linen cloth, made her own candles and, when cattle were first brought to Jamestown in 1615, she made her own butter and cheese. She kept a number of chickens, too, but appears to have shared the Chickahominy aversion to eggs, and although she served them to others, never ate them herself.

On September 15, 1615, one year after Pocahontas and

John Rolfe were married, they had a son, whom they named Thomas. Regarded as a symbol of the union of the Old World and the New, his birth was celebrated by the ringing of the bell recently installed in the steeple of the church. A few weeks earlier, Lord and Lady de la Warr had returned to England, and Sir Thomas Dale had become the first citizen of Jamestown. The new Governor and his lady were the baby's godparents when he was baptized in a ceremony held late in September. Soon thereafter the Reverend Mr. Hunt contracted an illness that forced him to go home to England, and his replacement did not arrive in the colony until the following spring.

Late in the autumn of 1615 Pocahontas and Rolfe took all three of their children on a visit to the main town of the Chickahominy. Few details of the visit are known, other than that Pocahontas donned Indian garb for the journey and Rolfe wore buckskins. But it must be assumed that an appropriate Chickahominy celebration was held, as the infant was the direct descendant of the Chief of Chiefs, and was entitled to receive the homage of his warriors. Mataoko had not seen his sister since she had been kidnapped by Captain Argall and taken to Jamestown, but he was present now, even though his relations with Pocahontas did not extend beyond necessary civilities. If ceremonies were held for the baby, Mataoko attended them, and it was his duty to march three times around the fire and, chanting an old song, to promise he would place his little nephew under his protection. In view of their later relations, it is likely that the ceremony was held; many years later Mataoko remembered his pledge—and kept it.

The visit lasted about a week, and the Rolfe family returned to Jamestown, escorted by a band of warriors. During the next two years, prior to her own departure for England, Pocahontas paid a number of other visits to the land of the Chickahominy, but no information is available regarding their frequency or what may have transpired there. It is probably a mistake to read deep significance into these trips. A young wife and mother went into the interior with her child and stepchildren to visit her family. Barbara Rolfe, who paid a number of visits to the Chickahominy, often was asked about these journeys after she became Lady Butler, but she had nothing to tell, regarding the trips as natural and normal. Like her brother and half-brother, she found nothing out of the ordinary in Indian living, and on one or two occasions she became annoyed when someone persisted in asking questions.

Pocahontas was determined to give her child and stepchildren the benefits of maternal love that had been so conspicuously lacking in her own childhood, and the women of Jamestown praised her, no one speaking more loudly on her behalf than Lady Dale. But Jamestown was upset by some of her habits, including that of bathing daily in the river, and taking the children with her. She observed the colony's taboos by wearing a man's shirt and trousers when she swam, but she refused to clothe the children, insisting the cleansing and healing properties of the waters would not benefit the youngsters if they were clad. Not even Lady Dale could persuade her to clothe the children when they swam.

Another of the Chickahominy practices observed by Pocahontas was that of going deep into the woods, alone, on the night of a full moon. No one in Jamestown knew what she did there, and on several occasions members of the colony followed her, hoping to keep watch on her. But they made so much noise in the underbrush that it was easy for her to shake them off.

Some colonists insisted that Pocahontas was observing various pagan rites, but she had become such a devout Christian that it is improbable she clung to any of the rituals of the Indians. Besides, there is no known Chickahominy rite that celebrates the full moon. What is true is that Chickahominy women frequently went into the fields under a full moon and sat cross-legged on the ground as they let the moon's rays rid them of their problems and restore their serenity. So it well could be that Pocahontas, whose life was full as a housewife, mother and family manager, found it a relief to escape alone into the open countryside for an evening of tranquility that would rid her of the petty annoyances of daily living.

Several large shiploads of immigrants reached Jamestown late in 1615. Most of the newcomers had been residents of the London slums, the Crown already having adopted the policy of shipping undesirables to the New World rather than clogging the prisons with petty criminals. These men and women were jealous and belligerent, felt no respect for authority or law and no kinship with those who enjoyed more comforts and privileges. They immediately resented the lot of Pocahontas: she lived in a fine home, while they were forced to dwell in miserable huts until they built dwellings of their own; she served unnumbered delicacies at dinner, while they were forced to subsist on parched corn and smoked meats until they either obtained employment in town or made their farms pay.

Pocahontas, these immigrants declared, was an intruder, and as a member of any Indian tribe was of a lower order than any Englishman, they demanded she be expelled from the community. According to a story that is undoubtedly apocryphal, Pocahontas challenged the newcomers by making a long, impassioned speech to them, thereby changing their attitude toward her and winning their support. At no other time in Pocahontas's life did she display boldness or become aggressive, and it is difficult to believe she would go alone before a group of hard-bitten cockneys in an attempt to win their friendship.

If the matter was handled as were similar problems, the newcomers were taken before Sir Thomas Dale and addressed in harsh terms. He told them, as he did Pocahontas's few other critics, that she was one of the colony's most distinguished and honored residents, that an insult to her would cause a war between the settlement and the Chickahominy Confederation, and that she and her husband were among his own friends.

John Rolfe needed more workers on his rapidly growing tobacco plantation, so he hired two of the new arrivals, paying them the same wages his other employees received. The more they saw of Pocahontas, the more they appreciated her character, and by the end of the winter they shared the admiration of everyone else in the colony for her. The opposition to her died away, and the incident is the only known cause of distress for her in the more than six years she lived in Jamestown. If her equanimity had been ruffled by the affair, it was soon restored.

In the main, the new immigrant was the least desirable of the types that came to the New World. He resented authority, tried to disobey orders, and not having had any desire to leave England in the first place, felt no desire to create a different life for himself in America. According to a report Sir Thomas sent to the Privy Council, the newcomers were "sly connivers, miserable fellows who quarrel with everyone and do no work unless they are threatened with starvation, until they produce their fair share of work."

The Privy Council did not reply to the Governor until the early spring of 1616, when he also received a letter from the directors of the London Company, and both communications were disheartening. The British Isles were enjoying a new era of prosperity, and even the Scots, traditionally poverty-stricken, had money in their pockets and enough food on their tables. Consequently, trained artisans and expert farmers were reluctant to abandon their improved state of affairs for the unknown wilderness terrors of the New World.

Neither the Privy Council nor the London Company directorate mentioned another important reason for the decline in voluntary migration to the New World. Books by Smith, Wingfield, Percy and others had appeared in print by this time, and all England soon realized that gold and gems couldn't be scooped up by New World travelers. Quite the contrary was true: anyone who went to America would have to work hard in order to survive, and would be unable to escape from the dangers of the wilderness.

So, the Privy Council concluded, in order to maintain the steady flow of immigrants that the growth and development of Virginia demanded, it was necessary to empty Newgate and other prisons. Many were lazy and would perish, but others would acquire the strengths they needed if they hoped to live, and in time they and their descendants would be honorable men and women of whom the Crown could be proud.

Sir Thomas Dale was worried only about Jamestown's immediate future, and was content to leave the colony's long-range prospects in the hands of others. He held a series of meetings with his subordinates, with the gentlemen and with those commoners who now qualified as men of substance and standing. They agreed that the survival of the colony depended upon an influx of the right kinds of immigrants, and that steps would have to be taken to persuade conscientious men and women to migrate to America.

Lord de la Warr, now in London, wrote he would be pleased to act as a recruiting agent for the London Company. Any assistance rendered by a man of his wealth and position would be valuable, but he was a patrician who had little to do with the lower classes. Therefore, even though he had lived long enough in Virginia to persuade his listeners that he was telling the truth when he extolled the New World's true wonders, he had too few contacts with the masses to be helpful on a large scale.

Something had to be done, and quickly, to prevent Jamestown from being transformed into a penal colony dependent upon large-scale, unremitting Crown assistance.

XVI

Jamestown's need for the right kind of immigrants was urgent, and Sir Thomas Dale has been credited with the idea of obtaining broad-scale publicity for the colony that would be beneficial. The plan was very simple: Pocahontas, her husband and their children would make a prolonged trip to England. Regardless of who originated the scheme, it fitted John Rolfe's plans perfectly. By 1616 he had become convinced that the new tobacco he had developed would earn a fortune, and he wanted to obtain private financial support for a major expansion of his holdings.

The personal curiosity of Pocahontas was also a major

153

factor in the decision to make the trip. The twenty-one-year-old girl had cast her lifelong lot with the English colonists, and she was anxious to see their homeland, especially the city of more than one million inhabitants, one of the largest on earth, a metropolis so vast it was beyond the reach of her imagination.

Sir Thomas and Lady Dale decided to escort the Rolfe family, and Sir George Somers became the acting Governor. The party sailed in the old *Susan Constant*, leaving Jamestown late in August, 1616. Commodore Newport resumed command of the ship for this one voyage. Pocahontas and her family were given luxurious accommodations, enjoying what was, in effect, a suite of cabins. They and the Dales ate their meals in the main saloon, and their own servants, who traveled with them, prepared and served their meals. Occasionally Commodore Newport joined them, but his relations with Sir Thomas had become somewhat strained in recent days, so he exercised the prerogative of a sea captain and ate most of his meals in his own quarters.

Pocahontas was the principal cause of the quarrel between the two men, Newport believing that Pocahontas was being exploited and that she would be out of her depth in England. Obviously Rolfe did not agree, as he could have prevented his wife from making the journey. Having determined that it was necessary for him to go to London, he may have been reluctant to leave his wife and children in the primitive community on the edge of the wilderness. It is inconceivable that Pocahontas could have come to harm at the hands of the Indians, but Rolfe may have felt less certain of the intentions of his fellow colonists, particularly the recent arrivals with prison records.

What the young woman may have thought on the long voyage can only be guessed. She was the first member of her nation to cross the Atlantic Ocean, and, to the best of her knowledge, the first of her race. It is unlikely that she felt any fears, as she was secure in the knowledge that her husband loved her and that she enjoyed the firm friendship of the Dales and of Lord and Lady de la Warr, who would act as her hosts during a portion of her sojourn in England. The sea could have held no terrors for her, either, because her faith in

God was so strong. But she must have wondered what kind of reception she would be given in a land so far removed from all she had known.

The education of the children was not neglected on the voyage. Pocahontas spent hours each day giving them religious instruction and quizzing them on their other work. She read a number of books, and, as usual, studied her Bible at length. She and Rolfe chatted with the Dales, and when the sea was calm, she was invited to the quarterdeck by Commodore Newport, who taught her the rudiments of navigation. Before the voyage ended she is known to have taken the wheel, much to her delight, and Newport gave her a certificate stating she had qualified as an able seaman. That document later became a possession of her son, and subsequently was passed down by his heirs.

The *Susan Constant* sailed up the Thames early in October, 1616, after an uneventful voyage. Word of her arrival had preceded her, and Lord and Lady de la Warr were on hand to greet the Indian princess and her family. Pocahontas was given a taste of what was to come when she came down the gangplank and saw a silent crowd of some hundreds of Londoners gaping at her. These men and women, attired in rough, simple clothes similar to that of Jamestown immigrants, reminded her of home, and she spontaneously smiled and waved. Most English aristocrats were reserved, taking no notice of the lower classes, and Pocahontas's unfeigned gesture of friendliness immediately won her the affection of the crowd. Cheers followed her as the party left the docks in several carriages.

How Pocahontas reacted to her first carriage ride, what she thought of the broad, cobbled streets, the massive stone buildings and the even larger Westminster Abbey and the House of Parliament is unknown. Subsequently she told Queen Anne she had been too numb to think.

Most of her first impressions must have been a blur. The town house of Baron de la Warr was located in the most fashionable part of London, off the Strand, not far from the site of present-day Covent Garden. The rooms were not large, but were elaborately furnished, and the tapestries on the walls, the thick rugs on the floors and the drapes of heavy, brocaded silk were unlike anything the daughter of Powhatan had ever seen. The suite that Pocahontas, Rolfe and their children occupied had its own bathroom, a luxury that only the wealthiest nobles could afford. In Pocahontas's bedchamber there were panes of clear glass in the windows, a miraculous innovation so new that some of the castles and palaces belonging to royalty were not yet equipped with them.

A crowd gathered outside the de la Warr house every day, cheering Pocahontas whenever she departed or came home. She always stopped to say a few words to those nearest her, and was cheerful in her demeanor, which endeared her to the throngs even more. Lord de la Warr would have ordered the crowds dispersed, but Pocahontas assured him she did not object and that she could understand their curiosity about her.

It quickly became apparent that her popularity had certain disadvantages, however. She had to be driven around town in a carriage on her sightseeing tours because people surrounded her when she tried to walk, jostling her, and both her husband and her host were afraid she might suffer personal injury.

Pocahontas's first days in London were devoted almost exclusively to sightseeing and to fittings by dressmakers who came to the de la Warr house. The few dresses that had been made for her by a Jamestown seamstress were unsuitable for a life in London's most aristocratic circles, so she needed a whole new wardrobe.

There were few callers other than the Dales at the de la Warr residence, but Pocahontas's sponsors were undismayed. The protocol of aristocratic London was complicated, and the great nobles of the realm lived in constant fear they would win the disapproval of the court if they made a false move or became friendly with someone King James or Queen Anne disliked. So no one wanted to act until he learned the reactions of the monarch and his consort, and neither the de la Warrs nor the Dales were in any hurry.

One of the ironies of Pocahontas's first days in London was that the house in which she lived was only a few city blocks from the lodgings of Captain John Smith. Smith, who probably had not yet learned of Pocahontas's arrival in

England, was at that time trying to obtain financial support for another voyage to New England, and was also trying to persuade various nobles that it would be profitable to establish a permanent colony there. In order to further those aims, he had just published a new book, *A Description of New England,* which had been registered at Stationers' Hall on June 3, the date of its publication.

The book was written in Smith's usual, flamboyant style, but his basic facts were accurate and the maps he included were precise. The book was already creating something of a stir in academic, scientific and aristocratic circles, but the wealthy were reluctant to invest in another of Smith's enterprises, his fiasco in 1615 having cost his backers large sums of money. His work would inspire the Pilgrims, currently living in Holland, to establish their colony in New England in 1620, but no men of substance were coming forward now with funds for a new venture. The death of Prince Henry, Smith's principal patron, had been a staggering blow, and the honors Smith had been given were empty.

His financial situation had become precarious. His inheritance was enough to pay only his rent, and he depended on the sale of his books for his living. Until now his work had enjoyed great popularity, enabling him to keep his mistresses in style, but he had invested some of his own funds into his last, abortive voyage. This had put him into debt, his creditors were demanding payment from him, and he had been forced to pledge them the better part of the royalties *A Description of New England* earned for him. The alternative was debtors' prison and disgrace.

So John Smith faced a critical situation. Months might pass before the publication of his new book helped persuade potential patrons to invest in a new expedition to New England. In the meantime he had to find new sources of revenue or cut down drastically on his style of living, a prospect that was displeasing to a man who liked good food and expensive blondes.

Meanwhile Pocahontas was becoming acclimated to London living. The weather was turning chilly, so Sir Thomas Dale had a cape of beaver fur made for her, shrewdly—and correctly—believing that her appearance in the cloak would stimulate an even greater demand for the furs of the New World. Few women could walk with grace in the stiff-soled shoes built on high platforms that were London's latest style, but Pocahontas was endowed with a perfect sense of balance, and soon was able to manage the footgear better than most, even though she shared the opinion of other ladies that they were very uncomfortable.

She had discovered that the food of the aristocracy was too rich for her. A lifetime of simple meals had made dishes served with rich sauces of wine and herbs and spices unpalatable, and she found, too, that she was physically incapable of consuming the many courses set before her. An ordinary dinner might include as many as eight or nine courses, and at least fifteen were served at banquets, each of them with its own wine.

Disliking wine and unable to eat most dishes, Pocahontas subsisted mainly on grilled meat and fish, boiled vegetables and such raw fruits as pears, peaches and grapes. As she would soon reveal, she was warned that, in the unlikely event she was asked to dine at Whitehall, royalty would be offended if she refused to eat any dish placed before her. But Pocahontas merely smiled and kept her own counsel, her sponsors in London society forgetting that she, too, was a member of a royal family.

Lady de la Warr and Lady Dale, who were supervising the making of Pocahontas's new wardrobe, were confronted by a vexing problem. Should they have gowns made for her that included some hint of Indian attire, or should they dress her exclusively in the latest London fashion? They wisely adopted the latter course, her figure being perfect for contemporary English fashions and for the monarch's own taste. The women in whom King James showed an intermittent interest were long-legged, had small buttocks and even smaller waists, high breasts, long necks and small heads.

King James always wore a wig in order to conceal his increasing baldness, so the court also went wigged, and the style had been adopted by the lesser aristocracy and the middle class. No one ever appeared at Whitehall in his own hair without suffering royal displeasure, and it may be that the coolness of King James toward Captain John Smith had stemmed, at least in part, from the refusal of the explorer to don a wig.

Pocahontas shared Smith's feelings on the subject, although it is improbable that she knew what he thought. She took pride in her waist-long hair, and although she was amenable in most matters, allowing Lady de la Warr and Lady Dale to tell her what gowns to wear and to order new clothes they deemed the most attractive, she balked when a wigmaker came to fit her. Under no circumstances would she wear a wig, even if it meant returning to Jamestown on the next ship that sailed to the colony.

Sir Thomas and Lord de la Warr must have suffered misgivings, wondering if they had been wrong to bring the Indian princess to London, and made even more strenuous efforts to persuade her to change her mind. Whether Rolfe also joined in the chorus is unknown, but Pocahontas remained adamant, calmly resisting the pressure applied to her. She was happy with her husband and children, and although she wanted Jamestown to flourish, she refused to be used in ways that were anathema to her.

Rolfe was already at work on his own behalf, trying to find sponsors for his projected enlargement of the tobacco-growing industry. One of those interested in what he had to say was Robert Carr, Earl of Somerset, who had been one of Jamestown's original sponsors. Somerset lived in a mammoth palace on the Strand, at the foot of Fleet Street, built for him by King James in the days when he had been the royal favorite. The King had cooled in his friendship, but Somerset was independently wealthy and had become one of the most prominent nobles in England and Scotland.

Lord de la Warr and Sir Thomas Dale encouraged Rolfe's relationship with the Earl for reasons of their own. Although Somerset came to court now only for meetings of the Privy Council and other state functions, King James remained jealous of him, and royal spies planted at Somerset House told the monarch about his former favorite's social life. Somerset knew, of course, that Rolfe was the husband of Pocahontas, and it was just a matter of time before the Indian princess received an invitation to one of Somerset's parties. His assemblies were far more elaborate than the frugal receptions held at the royal court, and most aristocrats eagerly awaited an opportunity to eat the French dishes prepared by the Earl's chefs, drink his fine wines and listen to the musicians who played on these occasions.

The assembly Pocahontas attended was held in mid-November, about a month after her arrival in London, and launched her social career with a roar. She was escorted by her husband, of course, and the de la Warrs and Dales were in attendance. Pocahontas wore a new gown of emerald velvet, with it diamond earrings and a diamond brooch from the de la Warr collection. Over her shoulders was her new beaver cape, which she discarded after making her entrance, and at least a dozen great ladies wrote exicted letters about her appearance as well as her personality and charm.

What made the greatest impression on the most powerful and wealthiest nobles of the realm was her ability to speak a perfect English with the accents of the aristocracy. Her grammar was as flawless as her poise, and she displayed the graciousness expected of a princess. The most influential men in the British Isles promptly fell in love with her, and their wives admired her so much that her hairstyle started a new fad. Within twenty-four hours every aristocratic London lady was wearing her own hair piled high on the crown of her head, held in place by tiny gold and diamond pins.

The Earl of Somerset knew he had scored a social coup, and within a few days—according to some accounts it was the very next day—he signed an agreement with Rolfe. Under the terms of this contract Somerset promised to match the funds Rolfe raised elsewhere for the enlargement of his tobacco plantations and the shipping of tobacco leaves to England. It could be argued that the canny Robert Carr knew an attractive business proposition when he saw one, and would have invested in Rolfe's enterprise in any event. But this does not take from Pocahontas the distinction of having made a major contribution to her husband's vocation—and to the future of the entire Virgina tobacco industry. Thanks at least in part to her triumph at Somerset House, the Earl quickly formed a lasting association with Rolfe.

Pocahontas overnight became the belle of London.

160

Various artists clamored for the honor of painting her portrait, and it has been assumed that several of them did versions of her likeness. Two of these works later came into the possession of Thomas Rolfe, but were improperly packed for transfer to the New World, and were crushed beyond repair when a storm caused a shift in the cargo stored in the hold of the ship in which they were being transported to America.

Thomas Heywood, a prominent playwright-actor-theatrical manager of the period announced that he was writing a new play that he intended to dedicate to Pocahontas, and the project received so much favorable advance publicity that Heywood then declared he would write a drama based on her life. If such a work was ever completed, it has been lost to posterity.

George Wither, a poet whose works were popular with the nobility of his day but who has been regarded in later centuries as a minor seventeenth-century literary figure, wrote a sonnet which he dedicated to Pocahontas, and it achieved great popularity when it was rushed into print as the first poem in a new book Wither was publishing.

William Browne, a poet who had family connections in high places, was present at Somerset House on the night Pocahontas made her social debut there, and was so inspired when he saw her that he wrote one of his better-known works, *Ode to a Lady*, for her. He was said to have called at the de la Warr house to present her with the original of the work.

Captain John Smith could not have failed to become aware of the commotion Pocahontas caused, and must have been dismayed. Jamestown would not have survived without his efforts, and he had been the first to establish relations with Powhatan. Had it not been for him, the daughter of the Chief of Chiefs would not have left her home in the wilderness, and under no conceivable circumstances would she have come to London. Yet he, an explorer of standing and an author of repute, had no part in her triumph, enjoying none of the benefits—at a time when his own financial needs were great. Obviously something had to be done to rectify this situation, and Smith began to ponder.

Meanwhile Pocahontas and Rolfe were amused by the

reception that social London accorded the Indian princess, and her head remained unturned. Lady de la Warr marveled at her calm.

Sir Thomas Dale and Lord de la Warr knew they had won the first round in their battle to launch Pocahontas and win greater popularity for Jamestown. But they realized, too, that their victory would not be complete until Whitehall reacted favorably.

XVII

Queen Anne, the consort of James I, may have been one of the most considerate and charming women of her day, as many of her friends and supporters claimed. Certainly she was one of the unhappiest.

She was the only daughter of Frederick II of Denmark, the "Warrior King" who steadily expanded his realm until his long war with neighboring Sweden drove both nations to the verge of bankruptcy. Frederick had little time for his daughter, instead expending most of his limited paternal feelings on his son, the charismatic crown prince who eventually became Christian IV. Anne spent much of her childhood alone, and tried to compensate for her loneliness by reading every book she could find. Certainly it was true that she was one of the best-educated women in Europe.

In 1589 the shy, homely Danish princess was married to James of Scotland, whom she had never met. Although he was the heir to the English throne of Elizabeth I, his prospects were regarded as dim, and King Frederick was subjected to considerable criticism for not marrying his daughter to someone who had better hopes of becoming a major ruler. But, when James succeeded to the throne of England in 1603, the wisdom of Frederick became self-evident, and Denmark signed a new treaty of alliance with England.

Queen Anne performed the duties required of her, and bore her husband three children: Henry; Charles, who would become Prince of Wales and eventually King; and Elizabeth, who would become the wife of Frederick V, the Elector of the Palatine and the most important Calvinist prince in all of the German states. It was rumored that James and Anne were secret converts to Catholicism, and if the reports were true—they are still being debated by present-day scholars—this formed one of the few genuine bonds in the marriage of the King and Queen.

Another real tie was their intellectualism. James loved to regard himself as a scholar and prose writer, and a collection of his works was printed in 1619. Anne had no such pretensions, but was far more widely read than her husband and was familiar with most of the writing of the period on theology, philosophy and poetry.

For the most part Anne tolerated her husband's many eccentricities with good grace. Kings were expected to take mistresses, and she could accept the women in James's life, but his occasional lapses into homosexuality distressed her, and she went to great pains to make certain her sons were not corrupted. She quietly ignored the King's ban on the use of firewood in the royal residences, and her apartments in Whitehall, Hampton Court, Theobalds and the other palaces were the only rooms that were warm. Her court was a separate institution, and James tolerated its existence because she permitted no political discussions there. James, whose early, stormy life had made him paranoid, was convinced that his nobles were conspiring against him and consequently never delegated much authority to any one subordinate over a long period, but he entertained no such suspicions about his wife.

Her court was far more popular than her husband's, and not only because the rooms were comfortably warm, the food edible and the wine the best that could be imported. Conversation was lively, scholars and men in the arts were frequent guests, and no one was excluded because of his opinions. Anne was willing to tolerate sexual promiscuity in others provided they were discreet, but she herself lived a chaste, highly moral life and tried to set an example for the ladies of the realm. Thanks in large part to her own standards, the court of James I was far less morally corrupt than it otherwise would have been.

Prince Charles, who was sixteen years of age at the time of Pocahontas's visit to England, was uncomfortable in the presence of his father and spent most of his time, when possible, at the court of his mother. He had been deeply devoted to his brother and sister, and the death of Henry in 1612, closely followed the next year by Elizabeth's departure for the Palatine, left him a lonely boy. Like his parents, Charles was an intellectual, and thanks to an alert governess and equally devoted tutors, he had been spared some of the wild ideas of his father, who had tried from time to time to dabble in his education.

Charles had no vices, and all who knew him believed he would become a model king. He abhorred homosexuality, accepted his mother's precept that even a ruler should remain monogamous and cared so little for wine that water was always added to his cup in generous quantities. He was studious, courtly and shy, spoke with a marked Scottish accent and was hampered until the tragic end of his days by a debilitating stammer when he became excited or was under pressure. No one ever heard him raise his voice in anger, and it was said he had such complete self-control that he never permitted himself to lose his temper. Physically he was slender, short and moved with a quick grace; he had a high forehead, wide-set eyes and laughed quietly.

Charles was passionately devoted to hunting and riding, and was a sincerely devout Anglican who tried hard to live according to the precepts of the church. A few years later he refused to marry a Spanish princess with whom he became infatuated because it would have become necessary for him to give up his own faith and embrace Roman Catholicism.

His defects did not become apparent until later years. He lacked imagination and was unyielding, often rigid in his views. Always defensive when the honor of the house of Stuart was questioned, he neither understood nor appreciated the democractic process of government, and his belief in the divine right of kings hardened as his disputes with the House of Commons became more intense. Unlike Pocahontas, he lacked curiosity about the world, was stiff in the presence of those he regarded as his inferiors, and at no time in his life did he have social intercourse of any kind with either the middle class or those he called "the rabble."

Charles became Prince of Wales only two or three weeks after the arrival of Pocahontas in England, but she did not accompany Baron and Lady de la Warr to the investiture ceremonies. Soon thereafter Queen Anne and her son learned of the triumph the Indian princess had achieved at Somerset House, and she received an invitation to a levee at Whitehall.

Lady Dale taught her how to curtsy, and on the appointed day she dressed in a low-cut gown of crushed yellow velvet, creating a minor crisis when she once again refused to don a wig. Escorted by her husband and flanked by the de la Warrs and Dales, she set out for Whitehall.

Some members of the Queen's court had already met Pocahontas at Somerset House and knew what to expect, but those who had never before seen her were dazzled. Queen Anne leaned forward on her throne to stare down at the girl who sank to the floor in a graceful curtsy. Then, when Pocahontas turned again to curtsy before the Prince of Wales, whose throne sat at right angles to that of his mother, the future Charles I suddenly came to life. He leaped off the dais, grasped Pocahontas by the hand and refused to allow her to curtsy; then he insisted that a chair be placed beside his, declaring that her rank entitled her to sit in his presence and that of his mother.

That was the beginning of Pocahontas's close

friendship with the next ruler of England, but the gossips who tried by innuendo to claim there was a romance between them were mistaken. The devout Pocahontas loved her husband, and it would have been out of character for the equally devout Prince of Wales to make advances to her. Charles was lonely, and in Pocahontas he found a royal personage of his own generation with whom he could relax.

The story of Pocahontas's first meeting with Queen Anne was told by a score of people, and most accounts were agreed on the principal points. Displaying no awe, the girl chatted with ease, but took care to show deference to Anne. She was far freer with Charles, making no attempt to curb her natural gaiety, and treated him as an equal, something that no one else in the realm dared to do. Baron de la Warr looked disconcerted, apparently fearing she would be rebuked, but his apprehensions were groundless. Queen Anne was charmed, and so was her son.

Before the levee ended, Pocahontas received an invitation to dine privately with the Queen the following day. A command appearance after such a brief acquaintance was unprecedented, and Sir Thomas Dale knew his gamble had succeeded beyond his greatest expecations. Unless an unforeseen catastrophe took place, minor aristocrats and untitled members of the gentry would fall over each other in their eagerness to go to Virginia and in that way win royal favor.

As Lady de la Warr later wrote in a vein of self-irony, she and Arabella Dale spent long hours trying to convince Pocahontas that she was required to eat anything placed before her at Whitehall. The Indian princess, who was devoted to her friends, smiled her customary, enigmatic smile and said nothing.

The following afternoon Queen Anne of England, consort of James I and only daughter of Frederick II of Denmark, dined alone with "Lady" Rebecca Rolfe, wife of John Rolfe, gentleman, and only daughter of Powhatan, Chief of Chiefs of the Chickahominy Confederation. The girl who only a few years earlier had squatted before a cooking pit, attired in a crude dress of buckskin, tearing roasted meat apart with her bare hands, sat at a handsome table, using a gold knife and fork and eating her superbly prepared food from a plate of solid gold.

The miracle of the occasion is that Pocahontas succeeded in winning the genuine affection of the Queen. Her manners, which were perfect, were of less importance to the Queen than her character, and Anne was deeply impressed. When Pocahontas later revealed that she had courteously refused rich dishes, Barbara de la Warr said she should have saved her breath.

No one has ever known precisely what the former Danish princess and the former Chickahominy princess discussed behind the closed doors of Queen Anne's private dining chamber, but the close relationship they established indicates they achieved a remarkable degree of rapport. Certainly Anne, like her subjects, never ceased to find it miraculous that a "heathen savage" should have become a cultured, polished Christian. What is still amazing to people who live three and a half centuries later is that Pocahontas should have proved so malleable and should have possessed the ability to make such a complete change in her appearance, manner and attitudes. Just as Jamestown had been a far cry from the land of the Chickahominy, so glittering Whitehall was even farther from the little English colony so precariously perched on the shores of distant Virginia. But the quiet girl managed each leap without faltering, and always landed gracefully on her feet.

All London was agog when Pocahontas recieved her third invitation to the palace only twenty-four hours after her second visit there, and even those who had assumed the Queen's interest in her was a passing fancy now knew better. On this occasion she was accompanied by Rolfe and their children. They were received in a private audience, and as was customary on such occasions, no information relative to the visit was ever revealed to outsiders.

Thereafter the Rolfe family frequently went to Whitehall, and many years later, after John the younger had become an official at the court of Charles I, he recalled that he had spent many of his childhood hours roaming through the corridors of the palace and, on one occasion, found himself in the throne room of King James, from which he fled with all possible haste.

On the Sunday after these visits Pocahontas and her husband accompanied Queen Anne and the members of her suite to Divine services at Westminster Abbey. They sat in the first row of the royal pews, and with the Queen took communion from the Archbishop of York, who officiated. Apparently the Archbishop had some advance notice of the membership of the Queen's party because his sermon was entitled, *The Devotion to God Shewn by the Great Ladies of the Realm.*

It has been said that Pocahontas's conversion to Christianity was the principal reason for her acceptance by Queen Anne and for all that happened thereafter. Had she not become a Christian it is unlikely that she would have made the voyage to England in the first place, but it was her charm, intelligence and wit that endeared her to the Queen and to the others who became so attached to her during her sojourn in London. Undoubtedly Anne was attracted to her because of her piety, Anne herself being a pious woman, regardless of whether she was an Anglican or had secretly embraced Catholicism. But many of the others who came to know Pocahontas and became sincerely devoted to her were worldly men and women who, if they attended church at all, merely paid lip service to religious conventions.

The Queen rarely accompanied her husband to Theobalds, his favorite among the royal residences, and instead often went to Hampton Court Palace, which Henry VIII and Elizabeth I had preferred. Soon after Pocahontas's friendship with Anne was formed, she and Rolfe began to receive invitations to spend a few days at a time at Hampton Court. A royal invitation could not be declined, and the couple went, but Pocahontas must have indicated to the Queen that the arrangement was not exactly satisfactory, and thereafter the Rolfe children also received frequent invitations. The older children played in the extensive formal gardens. Rolfe went hunting with some of the wealthy nobles of the Queen's suite, his increasing friendship with them better enabling him to obtain their pledges of support for the Virginia tobacco-growing industry that still existed mainly in his own mind. And Pocahontas spent at least a portion of each day in private conversation with the Queen.

A brief study of Anne's approach explains this seemingly extraordinary situation. The people of England, the Queen included, knew virtually nothing about the Indians of North America, but on the basis of the haziest of information regarded them as benighted savages and heathens, creatures who were little better than animals. But the young lady who had come to London was as cultured as any woman in King James's realm. She was better educated than most, and her intellect was the equal of the Queen's. Her manners were perfect, her attitudes totally acceptable, and she was a model Christian.

It could not have occurred to Anne that Pocahontas came from an astonishingly primitive civilization because life in the world of the Chickahominy was beyond the Queen's comprehension. Nor could she have understood that the father of the Indian girl could neither read nor write, lived in a primitive wilderness hut and led an existence unknown in even the most remote parts of Europe for almost two thousand years. The wildest forests Anne had ever seen were the woods near Hampton Court; when she walked on grass, it had been cut hours earlier, and when she sat in the shade of a tree, she could see its carefully pruned branches. Certainly she had never grown any flowers herself, much less cultivated vegetables or grains. Nor had she ever held a sewing needle in her hand and it is doubtful that she had ever set foot in a kitchen.

Perhaps she was told something of Pocahontas's previous life, but it was impossible for her to grasp the realities of day-to-day New World existence. She saw only what Pocahontas had become, not what she had been, and regarded her as a peer.

The Indian girl was a novelty, to be sure. Her skin was dark, her hair was blue-black, and the very fact that her background had been "different" gave her an exotic quality that made her a more interesting and exciting companion than any English or Danish noblewoman. Anne, like all queens, necessarily lived an isolated life; everyone she encountered deferred to her, and she was always conscious of the fact that she held a unique position. But Pocahontas was herself the daughter of a monarch, and consequently was Anne's equal.

Pocahontas's response to Queen Anne's friendship is far easier to understand. The girl's early life may have been primitive, but from childhood she had been aware that because she was the daughter of a ruler she stood apart from the ordinary person. So she could understand Anne's approach to life, grasp the essentials of the Queen's problems and sympathize with them. Once the two women had met, it was inevitable that a strong bond of kinship should develop between them.

XVIII

The friendship of Pocahontas with the Prince of Wales—in which John Rolfe was included and which was of enormous help to him in later years—was both simpler and more complicated than the relationship of the Indian girl and Queen Anne. Pocahontas's most prominent trait, one that was always mentioned at length by everyone who knew her, was her femininity. The future Charles I was a lonely adolescent, unable to establish a rapport of any kind with his eccentric father and forbidden by custom to remain close to his mother. The death of his brother and the departure of his sister from England had robbed him of peers, and he would reveal, years later, that at this stage of his life there was not one person in the realm who dared to call him by name or address him as an equal.

Pocahontas filled this gap in his life, and in effect became a highly satisfactory substitute for the sympathetic sister whose companionship he had lost. She not only listened to his problems but understood what he was saying and was able to give him advice that helped to ease his burden, even if she could not solve his dilemmas for him. Within a very short time she became his confidante, and his mother heartily approved.

In the years ahead Charles would become one of the great seventeenth-century patrons of the arts. At the age of sixteen he had already developed a keen and critical appreciation of painting, music and the theater, all of them aspects of culture in which his father displayed no interest. When he discovered that Pocahontas knew nothing about these subjects, he became her eager teacher.

Whitehall was not yet the art collector's paradise it would become, but its walls were lined with Renaissance paintings, and Charles delighted in taking Pocahontas on tours of the palace. They could be seen at various times of the day standing in a corridor before a portrait, the Prince explaining the style, content, symbolism and techniques in detail to his avid listener. He did the same on visits to Hampton Court Palace, and both were so assiduous in their study of paintings that members of the court could not resist making up private jokes about them.

Pocahontas also learned all Charles could tell her about tapestries, which were not only works of art but kept out the cold. Charles made her a gift of a Flemish-made tapestry depicting a scene in a medieval garden, and it later became the property of Thomas Rolfe, who gave it a place of honor in the drawing room of his Virginia plantation house.

The plays of the late William Shakespeare and of Ben Jonson continued to fill the theaters of London, and the works of new dramatists were appearing regularly, the popularity of the stage remaining undiminished in spite of the express disapproval of King James, who considered plays and players licentious. Prince Charles was an enthusiastic theatergoer, and took Pocahontas and Rolfe to a number of plays. Pocahontas was delighted, and when she attended a performance of *Macbeth*, her first, she was seen to place her hands over her face during some of the more gruesome scenes.

In time she developed critical faculties of her own. *The Merchant of Venice* and *Romeo and Juliet* were her favorites, and she attended several performances of each, applauding vigorously when she enjoyed an actor's performance.

Her presence in a theater created as much attention as did the play itself. She and Rolfe always sat with Prince Charles in the royal box, with the Indian princess placed at the side of the Prince of Wales. Audiences treated the future ruler of England with respect, standing when he entered his box, but the presence of Pocahontas created a far livelier atmosphere. People cheered when she arrived, and would not stop until she acknowledged the applause by smiling and waving. Rolfe and Charles appeared pleased on these occasions, and Pocahontas handled herself with aplomb. The cheers of the crowds did not upset her, and she appeared oblivious of the stares of the audience, many of whom watched her as much as they observed the performance on the stage.

When entering or leaving a theater, Prince Charles appeared to be unaware of his future subjects. His manner was not arrogant, he just did not notice the people who gaped at him. They were a part of a lifelong background he took for granted, and he was totally indifferent to them as human beings. Pocahontas, however, always treated crowds graciously. She smiled as people called out to her, often pausing to speak a word to a man or woman who said something that interested her.

London was quick to grasp and remember the idiosyncrasies of its celebrities, and people soon began to make deliberately provocative remarks in the hopes that Pocahontas would pause for an exchange of a few words. Lady de la Warr tried to break her of this habit, telling her it was beneath her dignity, but nothing deterred Pocahontas, and she continued to speak to those who addressed her. It was a habit that endeared her to the public, and when she and her family moved from the de la Warr town house to the Dale home in what is now St. James's, the crowds followed her there.

The Prince of Wales, as already noted, was an enthusiastic horseman, and it was his custom to go out every morning after an early breakfast for a brisk canter. On one occasion Pocahontas and Rolfe were invited to accompany him, and it was then that the girl suffered one of the few failures of her London sojourn. She had never before ridden a horse, and although a gentle mount was procured for her, she found it impossible to remain in the saddle.

For the first time in her life she showed distinct fear, and was obviously so uncomfortable that the outing was canceled; the experiment was not repeated. But there were unexpected results: Rolfe went riding with the Prince, and proved to be as expert in the saddle as Charles. They enjoyed an exhilarating ride, and thereafter John Rolfe was Charles's frequent companion on the trail.

As an outcome of the conversations they had on these rides, Charles developed a strong interest in colonization, and after his accession to the throne he actively encouraged the development of the American colonies. Virginia was his favorite, and when Thomas Rolfe took over the management of his father's tobacco plantations, King Charles made a personal investment in them.

The other Rolfe children also became closely associated with Charles. Barbara eventually married Sir Frederick Butler, an equerry on the staff of the King, who fought at Charles's side during the Civil War. After the monarch was dethroned and executed, the Butlers fled to France, remaining there in exile until the Restoration, in 1660, when Charles II became King. John the younger suffered a somewhat similar fate. He was a loyal follower of Charles I and commanded a regiment in the Civil War. He was wounded, and barely managed to escape from the country when the Roundheads of Oliver Cromwell took the rule of the nation into their own hands. He, too, went to France, where his share of the profits earned by the tobacco plantations in Virginia managed by his half-brother gave him a comfortable living. He never recovered completely from his injuries, and died in exile prior to the

Restoration, but his sons and grandsons achieved prominence at the courts of Charles II and James II. Certainly the whole family could trace its friendship and influence with the house of Stuart to the sympathetic understanding that Pocahontas showed Charles I when he was a boy of sixteen.

There can be little doubt that Charles felt completely at ease in the company of the girl to whom he referred in public as his "sister." Courtiers whose observation of the royal family was an occupation noted that Charles lost his stammer in her presence, and conversed fluently with her. He could have paid her no higher compliment.

By the early winter of 1617 Pocahontas had become one of the most prominent personages in London. Sir Thomas Dale and Lord de la Warr were ecstatic, as were the other directors of the London Company. Pocahontas had focused the attention of all England on the colony in Virginia, and more than two hundred prospective immigrants of the desired type had applied for passage on the next ship. Some were family men who would be accompanied by their wives and children, and although the Crown had not yet abandoned the policy of sending petty criminals to Jamestown, men of substance and character would far outnumber them.

Commodore Newport planned to return to the New World in April, and a second ship was purchased to carry the overflow of passengers. Sir Thomas and Lady Dale planned to sail on board the *Susan Constant*, probably in March, and would be accompanied by two hundred and seventy new settlers.

Pocahontas and Rolfe would remain somewhat longer, in part because the Indian princess was so effective as an agent of propaganda dissemination. There was an even more important reason for the prolongation of her visit to England: Sir Thomas and the directors of the London Company hoped she might—directly or indirectly—influence King James and persuade him to change his policy of sending prison inmates to Virginia. She had not yet been received by the monarch, who gave no indication he was aware of her existence, even though she had become so friendly with his wife and son. If necessary, she could work through Queen Anne and the Prince of Wales to persuade the stubborn James to change his mind, but everyone concerned believed it would be far better if she could make her approach to the King himself. The hope that an audience with him might be arranged was still strong, so she and Rolfe agreed to stay in England for several additional months.

It was at this time, in the early winter of 1617, that Captain John Smith created the legend that has linked his name with that of Pocahontas for more than three hundred and fifty years.

Whether Smith had met Pocahontas during her sojourn in London is not known, but his name appears nowhere in the letters, journals and diaries of the many people who took note of the girl's many activities. The failure to record such a meeting need not necessarily indicate it did not take place, but it does add another element of confirmation to the belief that they were not even acquainted.

It should be remembered that Smith had never met Sir Thomas Dale, and it was improbable that he had more than a passing acquaintance with Lord de la Warr, his successor as the chief executive officer of Jamestown. As a director of the London Company the Baron must have been familiar with Smith's reports from the New World, and it is probable that both he and Dale had read Smith's *True Relation* and *A Map of Virginia*.

One possible link was Commodore Newport, who had remained in England since bringing Pocahontas there. His precise whereabouts during these months are not known, and his name also does not appear in the lists of those who attended various functions. It should be remembered, too, that Newport's relations with the Dales had been strained during the Atlantic crossing.

On the other hand, Commodore Newport and Captain Smith had made the initial crossing to Virginia together in 1607, and until Smith's departure after his accident had been close associates and friends, each respecting the talents and attitudes of the other. So it is not unreasonable to assume that these old comrades had at least one reunion while Newport was in England. Even if Smith had learned of Pocahontas's presence in no other way—which is unlikely, in view of the publicity attending her visit—Newport would have told him about her.

The two men had far more in common than their mutual Jamestown past. Smith was making a supreme effort to send another expedition to New England and, if possible, to establish a colony there. The publication of *A Description of New England* in June, 1616, had created additional interest in the area, and he had obtained a measure of financial support for the enterprise. But the venture remained his own, and only through great nobles could he have obtained the immigrants who were so slow in coming forward, so he was on the verge of abandoning his plan to establish a colony.

His need for funds was still urgent when, in February, 1617, a new edition of *True Relation* was published. It was the custom of the era for an author to obtain possession of the loose, extra copies of the printed sheets that, when bound, comprised his book. That was undoubtedly the case in the present situation, as the printing was identical.

Printers in the seventeenth century did not necessarily fill every page with printing, and margins were erratic, with as much as three inches or more of white space appearing on some pages. In his new edition of *True Relation* Smith utilized these blanks by including a long footnote that ran from one page to the next.

That footnote was the story of his own alleged experience with Pocahontas, and in it he borrowed freely from the incident recorded by young Henry Spelman in *An Account of the Starving Time in Virginia*, which, it will be recalled, was published late in 1614.

According to the running footnote, Smith had been captured by the Chickahominy and, for reasons unmentioned, had been sentenced to death. He claimed that the execution was to have been carried out by the dropping of a heavy stone on his head. This alone makes his story suspect. The Chickahominy either killed their enemies by stabbing them or, in extreme cases, by means of slow torture. The idea of dropping a heavy stone was colorful and dramatic, but had no basis in fact.

The execution supposedly was prevented when

Pocahontas, as comely a young woman then as she was in the London of 1617, intervened. She threw herself on her knees before her father, and Powhatan, who loved her, granted her request. Smith strongly hinted that he had enjoyed a romance with Pocahontas, although he did not make the precise claim in so many words.

A study of the veracity of Smith's story must include an examination of certain facts. Spelman had said that the girl who had helped him had been a child. Smith made her a mature young woman whose age more or less coincided with that of the Indian princess who was creating such a sensation in London at the very time the new edition of the book was published. But the original edition of *True Relation*, in which there was no mention of Pocahontas, had been written and published in 1608!

At that time Pocahontas had been no more than thirteen years of age, and by no criteria, either of the English or her own people, could she have been old enough for romance. The case against Smith is conclusive, and many scholars have insisted there is no truth whatever to his story.

But John Smith never permitted accuracy to stand in his way. The new edition of *True Relation* sold out quickly, thanks to the inclusion of his fanciful tale about Pocahontas, and a third edition was printed in May, 1617.

By that time he had been compelled to make major changes in his personal plans. He still had enlisted no colonists for his New England settlement, and a continuing lack of funds made it impossible for him to carry on a full-scale recruiting campaign. He had acquired a fleet of three small ships, and decided to send them to the Newfoundland fishing banks, timing their arrival there with the advent of spring. They would obtain large quantities of cod, which would be salted on board, and would return without delay to England, where the sale of the fish would earn the investors a handsome profit. Then, their appetites having been whetted, it would be far easier for Smith to persuade them to invest more heavily in his proposed colony.

The ships sailed in early March, 1617. The new plan succeeded and the ships returned in August, while Pocahontas was still in England. Smith paid his investors a profit, and within the next year published yet another book, *New England's Trials*, the sole purpose of which was to persuade various nobles of the feasibility of establishing a permanent colony in that part of the world. Due to various vicissitudes, the funds were not raised, and Smith abandoned his project. When he did not accompany the Pilgrims to the New World in 1620, he gave up all hope of personally taking part in the establishment of another colony, and thereafter he supported himself exclusively with his writing.

The most important of his books appeared in 1624, and was called *The Generall Historie of Virginia, New England and the Summer Isles.* It was a long, detailed account of the New World, and included vast quantities of geographical data of enormous value. The book won universal recognition as a masterwork, and enabled Smith to take his place among the leading scholars of England. It might be added that the establishment of the Massachusetts Bay colony in 1629 was the direct outgrowth of the interest aroused by the publication of the *Generall Historie.*

Smith's accuracy in describing the land, the rivers and lakes, the mountains, the vegetation, the wildlife and the weather was not matched by a regard for the truth in dealing with his own exploits. His old insecurities revealed themselves again, and his personal history was a mixture of fact and fantasy in which he presented himself as a hero of great strength, intrepidity and cunning who won every battle with human adversaries and with the forces of nature. These sentimental, swashbuckling tales were overlooked by his contemporaries because of the fundamental solidity of his work.

In the *Generall Historie* he repeated the story he first told about himself and Pocahontas in the 1617 edition of *True Relation*, but he added a few embellishments to make the tale even more romantic and dramatic.

As soon as the legend came into being in 1617, other writers tried to win popularity for themselves by adding to it. A minor pamphleteer named Mumbaugh produced a fanciful little work in the summer of 1617, in which he claimed that Smith had been responsible for Pocahontas's conversion to Christianity. According to this tale, Smith first introduced her to worship services in the Jamestown church, and thereafter guided her study of Christianity in spite of the violent objections of her father and brothers. Not even Smith himself made any such claim.

No one called John Smith a liar until many years after his death, his contemporaries respecting his skill with a sword and his ability to use a pistol. The first to suggest he had allowed his imagination to overcome his regard for the truth was the Reverend Thomas Fuller, whose posthumously published book, *The Worthies of England*, was edited by his son and published in the 1660s, after the Stuart Restoration.

It is astonishing, however, that no one pointed out the discrepancies in the *Generall Historie* embellishments. In his 1624 book Smith wrote that Powhatan set him free on condition that he make the Chickahominy gifts of two cannon and a millstone. A party of warriors accompanied him to Jamestown to take possession of the guns—and to kill him at once if he failed to keep his promise.

Smith said the settlers, who had given him up for dead, rejoiced when he appeared in the colony. He explained what had happened, and his comrades helped him fill two mammoth demiculverin with stones. These cannon, he said, were the largest in the colony. He fired them with stunning effect, the stones crashing deep in the forest, where they demolished a number of trees. The warriors were badly frightened, but were even more afraid of Powhatan's anger, so they tried to cart away the cannon. The terrifying weapons were too heavy, however, and the Chickahominy returned to their home empty-handed. Apparently they forgot all about the millstone they had also been promised.

This story, although colorful, was nothing but gibberish, and anyone who had been in Jamestown in the colony's early days must have known it. In the first place, artillery bore the primary responsibility for the security of Jamestown, and the colonists would not have permitted the Chickahominy to haul away their guns, no matter what Smith might have promised under duress. No one knew the value of the cannon better than Smith himself, and it is inconceivable that he would have gone through the motions of keeping his word, regardless of what he might have said to Powhatan.

The mere mention of demiculverin was ludicrous. This piece, which was usually mounted on a warship, was as cumbersome as it was huge. Made of iron and brass, it weighed between four thousand and five thousand pounds, and was capable of firing a nine-pound shot about one thousand yards. What was more, the two demiculverin mounted in the Jamestown fort had been carried ashore from the *Susan Constant* under the most exasperating of conditions. Twice the special hoists that the colony's carpenters made for this purpose broke, and one of the guns fell into the James River, the accident creating a salvage problem that had taken several months to solve. Under no circumstances could a small party of warriors have carried the guns off through the forest, and any Chickahominy who had seen them knew it. None of the other accounts of Jamestown's early days mentioned the alleged incident, any more than they related the supposed Pocahontas romance.

Whether the 1617 edition of *True Relation* and Mumbaugh's pamphlet were called to the attention of Pocahontas is not known. If she saw the stories, however, she probably was amused by them. At the time these accounts were written she had achieved the pinnacle of her social success in England. She had learned to shrug off rumors that the Prince of Wales was in love with her and the even more vicious gossip that insisted she was having an affair with the dashing Earl of Buckingham. Neither Smith nor Mumbaugh traveled in her exclusive circle, and if she learned of Smith's tale, she must have thought it harmless.

Some of the London Company's directors still entertained a low opinion of Captain John Smith, and if Lord de la Warr and Sir Thomas Dale read the running footnote in *True Relation*, their contempt for Smith was confirmed. Certainly they knew that no useful purpose could have been served by denying his tale. On the contrary, inasmuch as they had brought Pocahontas to London to publicize Jamestown, anything that might appear in print about her was helpful.

During Pocahontas's sojourn in England Smith was living openly with one of the most notorious courtesans in England, Barbara Courtenay. Making no attempt to conceal the relationship, he appeared with her in public everywhere.

A buxom blond who had been disowned by her family when she had launched her life of sin, Barbara had engaged in previous affairs with a number of prominent men who had no desire to be reminded of their past association with her, and the doors of people of standing were closed to her. It is true, of course, that Smith could have gone out without her if he had intended to meet Pocahontas, but the mere fact that he was Barbara's acknowledged lover placed him under a social cloud, too.

According to a story that has been unverifiable for more than three and a half centuries, Pocahontas and Smith met at a reception given in the home of Baron and Lady de la Warr after she and her husband returned there from the house of Sir Thomas and Lady Dale in the spring of 1617. Many versions of this supposed meeting have been told by imaginative authors. According to one of the most popular, Pocahontas and Smith admitted to each other that they still loved each other, but said a sad, final farewell in order to preserve her marriage, family life and reputation. Such an incident could have had no basis in truth.

A still wilder account had it that Smith still loved Pocahontas, but that the success she had enjoyed had gone to her head and she treated him rudely. He had retreated, never trying to see her again, and because of her rebuff abandoned all future attempts to make another voyage to the New World.

Pocahontas was the heroine and Smith the villain of a third popular story: he tried to embarrass her by recalling their love in the presence of her husband, but she courageously told Rolfe the truth, and he ordered the discomfited Smith to leave the house at once. All of these tales are absurdly romantic inventions.

It is possible that Smith was a guest at the reception held in Pocahontas's honor in the de la Warr town house in May, 1617. The part he had played in Jamestown's early history was well known, and although he was viewed with a somewhat jaundiced eye by many nobles, he had nevertheless been given the title of Admiral of New England by King James, so he was anything but a nonentity. Since Pocahontas and Smith had not known each other in the New World their discussion, if any, could not have been personal. At most he could have told her he had known her father, and both might have marveled at the mention of Powhatan in a setting so far removed from the forests of the Chickahominy.

But the best of legends never die, and the story of the romance of Pocahontas and Smith is immortal.

XIX

James I of England and VI of Scotland may have been the monarch of all he surveyed, but even the few friends he had not alienated by 1616 and 1617 readily admitted that he was his own worst enemy, and that he habitually compounded his own problems. He was embroiled in a serious dispute with the Church of Scotland, insisting that such Anglican rites as confirmation by bishops and kneeling at communion be adopted. He elected to rule England without summoning Parliament into session, thereby incurring the enmity of the Commons, and he so completely failed to understand finances that he had already more than doubled the national debt left by Elizabeth I. His sale of monopolies was systematically ruining England's trade, her lifeblood. He quarreled violently with the Chief Justice, the brilliant, independent-minded Sir Edward Coke, and in 1616 he astonished and dismayed everyone who had a regard for English justice by dismissing Coke from office.

James's lack of judgment in his choice of subordinates to whom he gave high office was extraordinary. A number of scandals, including the divorce of the Countess of Essex and the murder of Sir Thomas Overbury, occurred during the period that the Earl of Somerset stood at the right hand of the King, and the public outcry was so great that James had been forced to dismiss Somerset from office.

The new royal favorite was George Villiers, one of the most handsome, ruthless, self-serving men of his time. Still in his early twenties, he had already been made Earl of Buckingham and soon would be elevated to the rank of Duke. A man of considerable talents, Buckingham wanted to become England's greatest statesman and administrator, but was forced to spend so much of his time listening to James showing off his erudition that he was severely handicapped. Not until the reign of Charles I, with whom he established a close friendship when the Prince of Wales was still a boy, did he achieve his ambitions.

Buckingham was generous, courageous and competent as well as handsome, but his nature was imperious, he was impetuous and careless of detail, and his ambitions made him reckless. Certainly his influence was a major factor in the disputes with the Commons that led to the Civil War.

By early 1617 James was playing with fires he could not control. He had already come under the influence of the Spanish ambassador, at whose insistent suggestion he would execute the still-popular Sir Walter Raleigh the following year. And subsequently he would outrage English public opinion by trying, through Spain—England's most hated enemy—to become the mediator in the Thirty Years' War.

In his person James was almost painfully unprepossessing. He was so miserly that only on the most formal of state occasions could he be persuaded to dress in silk and ermine, and under no circumstances would he permit new clothes of expensive materials to be made for him. It was said he never replaced the moth-eaten robe of ermine he wore to his coronation. His usual attire was a doublet and breeches of "mean wool," dark gray or black, and members of the court said privately that he reminded them of the rector of a poor country parish. His stockings were of heavy wool, and he preferred carpet slippers to shoes, even wearing slippers in his throne room. His wig was thick and heavy, presumably to ward off the cold, and he frequently jammed a battered, unornamented black hat on his head.

His diet made him painfully thin, but his reliance on bread gave him a paunch in his later years, and the Dutch ambassador wrote to The Hague that only the paunch prevented the King's sword-belt from slipping down to his ankles. The sword he habitually wore was plain, and was like the dress weapons that middle-class merchants carried as they went about their daily business.

The meals served at the King's table were notoriously wretched, and, as previously noted, members of the court ate with him only when they wanted a favor or could not find an excuse to absent themselves. James ate the cheapest cuts of meat, liked the herring that was a staple of the poor Londoner's diet and would not tolerate the expenditure of funds for rich sauces, imported delicacies or expensive wines. It was said that he personally examined the household bills paid to butchers, greengrocers, bakers and other tradesmen by the royal steward.

James was anything but regal. His Scottish accent was coarse. A dribble of spittle usually fell from the right corner of his mouth, and he wiped his running nose with the back of his hand. Believing himself an author and scholar of distinction, he delivered long daily lectures on any subject that happened to come into his head. The members of his court were not only required to listen to him by the hour, but were forced to admire and applaud his erudition and wisdom. These sessions were substitutes for genuine, hard work because His Majesty, in addition to his other faults, was lazy. In all, James was one of the most unattractive rulers in the long history of the English monarchy, but his power was absolute and he made almost all major and many minor decisions himself, delegating little authority to others. Another seven or eight years would pass before he would allow his son and Buckingham to administer the affairs of state.

At the time of Pocahontas's visit to London the King was supremely indifferent to the activities of his wife and son, and it would not have been unusual had he failed to grant an audience to the Indian princess. But Buckingham was already becoming friendly with the Prince of Wales, who not only sang Pocahontas's praises but arranged her introduction to the Earl.

Buckingham succumbed to her charm, as had everyone else in London. It is possible, even probable in the light of his character and in view of the furious gossip that ensued, that he made advances to her, it being his custom to engage in an affair with every attractive woman he met. But Pocahontas was virtuous and spurned him, which was unique in his experience since the beginning of his rise to power, and he was so deeply impressed that he told the King about her.

James, who had ignored whatever had been said about her by others, listened with care to anything his favorite discussed, and in late March of 1617 he demanded that Pocahontas be brought to him. Lord de la Warr undoubtedly spent many hours coaching Pocahontas for the audience; James was easily offended, and everyone who dealt with him at one time or another knew that certain subjects were to be avoided. Among them was religion, on which he regarded himself as an authority, and it was said he sometimes actually believed that he himself, rather than the scholars he had commissioned, had made the new translation of the Bible. Any mention of poetry was also taboo, the King having published a critical analysis of contemporary poetry some years prior to his accession to the throne of England.

Pocahontas was presented to King James on March 31, 1617, and a larger number of nobles than usual crowded into the throne room, braving the cold and steeling themselves for a royal harangue. So there were many who witnessed the meeting, and most of their accounts agreed on the details.

Pocahontas's beauty made no visible impression on James, and her charm left him as chilly as the walls of the

rone room. He initiated the conversation by asking her
ction to the architecture of London, and he was astonished
en she replied at length and in detail, discussing the
ferences in the construction of various churches and other
jor buildings. Here, it appeared, was a woman of intellect,
l the King decided to challenge her. He said he had heard
was a convert to Christianity, and demanded to know if
was familiar with any portions of the Bible.

She accepted the challenge, throwing Lord de la Warr's
ning to the proverbial winds, and quoted a long passage
from Genesis. Then, scarcely pausing for breath, she recited
two Psalms from memory, and ended her impressive
performance by quoting from the Gospels of Matthew and
John. All of the citations were taken verbatim from the Kir
James Bible.

There was a stir in the throne room, and James hims
appeared dazed. Scarcely able to believe what was happening,
he asked for additional quotations, citing passages from
various Books that were among his favorites. Pocahontas
complied, and her recitation was letter-perfect.

King James was so impressed that he invited her to dine
with him, which was extraordinary, and the courtiers felt
sorry for her. When one ate alone with the King, it was
impossible to send a full plate back to the kitchen. But the
members of the court wasted their pity. The plain foods,
plainly cooked, suited Pocahontas's palate, and she thoroughly
enjoyed the meal, perhaps the first she had liked in England.
Others gagged on the grilled herring and boiled mutton that
were among James's favorite dishes, but Pocahontas was
delighted to accept second helpings. And James, who had seen
great nobles squirm and gag as they ate his food, knew her
pleasure was genuine.

She was not offended, either, by the personal
mannerisms that so many of his subjects found offensive. She
had seen far worse in the land of the Chickahominy, where
handkerchiefs were unknown and warriors wiped their greasy
hands on their bare chests while eating. It is probable, too,
that Pocahontas felt genuine sympathy for him. Her father
had been isolated and lonely, too, and she knew how difficult
it was for a man in James's position to trust any of his

subordinates, who flattered and praised him no matter what he said or did. On a later occasion, when Prince Charles, Buckingham and a number of others were present, Pocahontas was actually heard to contradict one of the King's more inane remarks. Anyone else would have incurred James's lifelong enmity, but she was so gentle, so obviously lacking in malice that he happily accepted the correction.

Before the day ended the news traveled swiftly from one end of London to another, and foreign ambassadors sent hastily written reports to their own capitals: James I had found a new favorite. At no time was it suggested that Pocahontas had become his mistress, however. Ordinarily he preferred older women, but her youth would not have been a barrier, nor would her marriage, for the King showed a splendid disregard for that institution when he wanted a woman. It was the attitude of Pocahontas that set the tone of the relationship, and James became her friend, not her lover.

There could be no doubt that she pleased him, and at his express invitation she came to the throne room two or three days each week. One day, in the hearing of Lord de la Warr and several others, he offered to make John Rolfe a viscount or baron so she would have a title. Pocahontas reminded him that she was already a princess, and James broke precedent by offering her a long apology. No one could remember a previous occasion when he had begged anyone's pardon.

Two of the subjects Pocahontas discussed with him most frequently were religion and poetry, which wise courtiers habitually avoided, and her reputation in noble circles became even greater. She could do no wrong, it appeared, and had performed a miracle by taming the intractable Scotsman.

James personally arranged Pocahontas's celebrated meeting with a number of the Oxford and Cambridge scholars who had translated the new Bible. They sat at a long table in the chamber ordinarily used for Privy Council sessions, and the scholars were as astonished as the King had been by her remarkable knowledge of the Bible. Only her background in Biblical history was weak, but the questions she asked were perceptive, and she quickly grasped and assimilated everything she was told.

The meeting was so stimulating that, at the command of the King, a number of subsequent sessions were held. James attended all of them, enjoying himself so much that he held his garrulity in check, and most of the talking was done by Pocahontas and the scholars. Irreverent courtiers privately joked that she would become the first Indian and the first woman to be made a bishop of the Anglican Church.

Thanks to James's interest in Pocahontas, John Rolfe was received in audience, and held several meetings with the King. It was he who managed to persuade James to alter his policy and stop sending convicted felons to Virginia. The relief was temporary, however, and again was changed during the reign of Charles I, when criminals were sent to virtually all of the American colonies as indentured servants.

James's abhorrence of tobacco was apparent to anyone who had read his published treatise on the subject, but the monarch loved money more than he hated any human vice, and Rolfe's talk of the profits to be made from "green gold" whetted the royal appetite. In June, 1617, James signed a patent granting John Rolfe the right to establish as many tobacco plantations as he wished in the royal colony of Virginia. Tobacco leaves would be carried to England in ships chartered privately, the funds for this purpose to be supplied by the Crown. In effect, King James made himself John Rolfe's partner, and the future of the tobacco-growing industry in Virginia was assured. The granting of this patent also assured the survival of Virginia, and she became economically self-sufficient before any other colony, except that of the Pilgrims at Plymouth, was even established.

During the spring and summer of 1617 Pocahontas was seen frequently in the company of the Earl of Buckingham at the theater and various social functions, so it was only natural, especially in view of Buckingham's reputation, that it should have been said she had become his mistress. But the gossips, deliberately for the sake of a good story, perhaps, ignored or forgot two important matters. First, John Rolfe was always present on these occasions, and was an honorable man who would not have closed his eyes to his wife's affair for the sake of convenience or his own profit. Second, Buckingham was always accompanied on these excusrions by one of the flashily attractive, ambitious young women, usually members of the minor aristocracy, whom he habitually made his mistresses. No evidence was ever presented, at the time or later, to indicate that Buckingham ever became Pocahontas's lover. There can be little doubt that he would have been willing, but for her to have indulged in an affair would have been completely out of character. Lady de la Warr, who would have been in a position to know of any indiscretions Pocahontas had committed, continued to marvel, praising her virtue and integrity, and so did everyone else who had become the friend of the Indian girl.

No better proof of Pocahontas's incorruptibility is needed than her continuing close association with Queen Anne, who had instilled a high moral standard in her son, and who permitted no licentiousness at her court. Had Pocahontas's conduct really been scandalous at any time she would have been dropped instantly by the Queen. Instead their friendship became even closer, and in September, 1617, Anne presented her friend with an emerald and diamond ring of great value, which later became a precious heirloom in the family of Thomas Rolfe. The Queen did not object to the association of Charles with the Earl of Buckingham, to be sure, but those who made it their business to observe such things were quick to note that Buckingham was rarely received by the Queen, and that on the rare occasions when he came to her court her manner was formal and chilly, obviously disapproving.

By the early autumn of 1617 Pocahontas, Rolfe and their children had spent the better part of a year in London, and the sojourn had been even more successful than Lord de la Warr and Sir Thomas Dale had dared to hope. Rolfe was anxious to return to Virginia and begin work on the expansion of the tobacco plantations, and Pocahontas was eager to go home, too. The swift pace of the social life she had endured without complaint for so many months was taking its toll, and for the first time she admitted to Lady de la Warr that she was tired. She had achieved an unprecedented triumph, not only conquering one of the most powerful nations on earth but helping to insure the survival of the Jamestown colony, and she was entitled to a rest. Her work was done, and she deserved a return to the relatively uncomplicated life that she and her family enjoyed in Virginia. She undoubtedly missed her own relatives, too, and must have yearned for a visit to the land of the Chickahominy.

According to Lady de la Warr, Pocahontas had a nightmare one night in September, and her screams awakened the entire household. The girl was obviously terrified, but would tell no one what she had dreamed; she could only beg her husband to take her back to Jamestown as soon as arrangements could be made.

XX

Commodore Newport returned to England after delivering Sir Thomas and Lady Dale to Jamestown, bringing with him a cargo of the New World's raw materials. Tired of a life of constant travel, he intended to retire and settle down on a small estate in Sussex, but he immediately agreed to make one more voyage to Virginia for the purpose of taking the Rolfe family home. A cargo of the supplies the settlers always needed was hastily purchased and stored in the hold of the reliable *Susan Constant*, and plans were made for a sailing in early October.

But Pocahontas's many friends had other ideas, and so

many farewell receptions and dinners were given in her honor that the sailing had to be delayed. The culmination of the festivities was a royal banquet held in the vast Whitehall chamber reserved for that purpose, and the Indian princess was seated on the dais with James, Anne and Charles. More than three hundred lords and ladies attended, and innumerable toasts were offered to the health and happiness of Pocahontas, John Rolfe and their children. Even little Thomas was there for a time, a governess taking care of his needs.

King James wore his robes of state for the occasion, and both the Prince of Wales and the Earl of Buckingham donned their recently bestowed blue ribbons of the nation's highest decoration, the Order of the Garter. Pocahontas was attired in a gown of ivory-colored satin which was trimmed with ermine tails, a fur reserved for members of royal families. She looked lovely, as always, and the entire company applauded when she entered on the arm of Prince Charles.

Close observers noted, however, that she seemed somewhat indisposed. There was a gray cast to her dark skin and her eyes lacked their customary luster. She ate little, but everyone knew she disliked rich foods, so her lack of appetite was not regarded as significant. Nevertheless, she displayed her usual animation, laughing and chatting with Queen Anne and Prince Charles, and holding a spirited but more sober conversation with King James.

On November 2 Pocahontas stunned London society by paying a visit to the imprisoned Sir Walter Raleigh in the Tower of London. Only a very few of the most powerful nobles dared to risk the King's displeasure by visiting the Great Admiral, but many regarded him as a martyr, and his already enormous popularity had increased during the long years of his incarceration. Pocahontas spent the better part of the afternoon with Raleigh, and although nothing specific is known of their discussions, it is likely that she answered many of his questions about life in the New World. All England applauded her considerate gesture, and even King James could not protest too strenuously. Raleigh's efforts had made the settlement of Jamestown possible, and Pocahontas was living proof of the farsightedness of the program of discovery and colonization that he had sponsored.

On November 5 Pocahontas and Rolfe attended a special communion service at Westminster Abbey, and were joined by Queen Anne, the Prince of Wales and the Earl of Buckingham. Most of the friends the couple had made in their thirteen-month visit were on hand, too, and the assemblage listened to a sermon delivered by the Reverend James Montagu, Bishop of Winchester, the royal family's favorite clergyman.

Thereafter Pocahontas and Rolfe rode to Whitehall, where they took their leave of King James in a brief audience. Then they returned to the de la Warr house for a farewell dinner. Pocahontas felt faint, and it was assumed that she was overcome by the excitement of leaving England and returning to Virginia. Apparently her indisposition was not deemed sufficiently serious to warrant the summoning of a physician.

Lord and Lady de la Warr accompanied their guests to the *Susan Constant*, and a large, noisy crowd of loyal Londoners was on hand to roar their goodbyes to the girl who had become as much the favorite of ordinary citizens as she was of the royal family and the nobility. Pocahontas waved, smiled and exchanged a few words with those nearest the gangplank, but her efforts were feeble, and everyone seemed to take it for granted that her leave-taking made her sad.

Commodore Newport gave the order to weigh anchor and cast off soon after sundown, and the *Susan Constant* took advantage of the evening tide as she sailed down the River Thames. Pocahontas was not on deck for a last glimpse of the London she had conquered, her weariness forcing her to retire immediately. Newport later wrote she had fallen asleep, so he and Rolfe dined without her.

Pocahontas did not awaken, and soon after dawn on the morning of November 6, 1617, she died in her sleep while the *Susan Constant* sailed westward through the English Channel, within sight of land. She was twenty-two years of age.

Even if the stunned John Rolfe had wanted to take her body back to the New World it could not have been preserved on a journey that would have taken six to eight weeks at that season of the year. So Commodore Newport turned back and cast anchor at the nearest town, Gravesend, a river port located on the right bank of the Thames, about Twenty-two miles from London.

A messenger was dispatched to carry the shocking news to London, and the following day a large party from the capital arrived in Gravesend, led by Queen Anne and Prince Charles, who joined John Rolfe, his children and Lord and Lady de la Warr in the mourners' pew for the last rites.

The funeral was held in St. George's Church, Gravesend, later called St. George's Chapel of Unity, on the morning of November 8, and Pocahontas was buried in the church, where her grave remains to the present day. The service was conducted by Bishop Montagu.

The crushed Rolfe, for the second time a widower, postponed his own plans to return to Virginia, went back to London and remained there for more than another year. He spent a short time with Lord and Lady de la Warr, then rented a nearby house for himself and his children.

He finally returned to Virginia in January, 1619, after sending the elder children to school in London and leaving Thomas in the care of a competent governess. Once in Jamestown he initiated his plan to build the tobacco-growing industry, and he worked unceasingly on the project for the next three years, by which time a number of large, prosperous plantations had been established.

Soon after his arrival in the late winter or early spring of 1619, Rolfe paid a visit to the main town of the Chickahominy and told Powhatan and his sons the sad news of Pocahontas's death. He is known to have paid a number of additional visits to the land of the Chickahominy thereafter, but the passage of time has obscured the details. Piaoko, Pocahontas's favorite brother, returned the visits and became a guest in the house of his brother-in-law, no longer insisting on sleeping in the open.

Rolfe returned to London in 1623, and by that time he was a wealthy man. Powhatan had died in 1618. Mataoko was the new Chief of Chiefs, and the long peace that his father and Captain John Smith had established was ruptured by the massacre of 1622. According to some authorities, though not conclusive, Rolfe was killed in this massacre. For two years thereafter the colonists and the Chickahominy waged an intermittent but bitter war. Both Jamestown and the main town of the Chickahominy were subjected to a number of attacks. No prisoners were taken by either side, however. The outlying plantation houses of the settlers were burned and their fields were laid waste, but the plantation belonging to John Rolfe was untouched.

Eventually exhaustion forced both sides to terminate the conflict, but the colonists were the winners, as Mataoko abandoned his capital and built a new town further inland, at the falls of the James River. This was the first of several moves, the pressures of increasing colonization driving the Indians ever deeper into the interior and ultimately causing the disintegration of the Chickahominy Confederation.

John Rolfe returned to Virginia in 1626 and remained there for two years. Again he took the leading role in the expansion and solidification of the tobacco-growing industry. He went back to England in the autumn of 1628, and never again left the country. After the death of Pocahontas he retired from English society, but remained on the friendliest of terms with Charles I, who became King in 1625, and with the Duke of Buckingham. He is also known to have been received during his earlier stays in England in private audiences, from time to time, by his business partner, King James.

Rolfe purchased a country house near Gravesend, and lived there in retirement. He recieved large, regular payments from the overseer he had left in charge of his Virginia plantations. At no time did he reply to the romantic story that Captain John Smith wrote about Pocahontas in his *Generall Historie.* The devout Rolfe regularly attended worship services at St. George's Church, Gravesend, often accompanied by one or more of his children, and as regularly visited the grave of Pocahontas.

John Rolfe the younger was graduated from Oxford University, and in 1629 entered the service of King Charles. The following year Barbara Rolfe was married to Sir Frederick Butler, baronet, a member of the household of the King. In the same year Thomas Rolfe was enrolled as an undergraduate at Oxford. In 1632 John Rolfe died, leaving his English business interests to his elder son, the Gravesend house and several other country properties to Barbara and a controlling interest in the Virginia plantations to Thomas.

In 1633 Thomas Rolfe was graduated from Oxford and took up the life of a gentleman in London. He was offered a place on the household staff of King Charles, who had fond memories of his mother, but Thomas Rolfe already had planned a far different life for himself, and declined.

A short time later, in the summer of 1634, he went to the Virginia he had left as a baby and took up residence in the plantation house built by his father. In the years following, the estate was vastly enlarged under his astute management. By the time he returned to the land of his birth, Jamestown, located on low, swampy land injurious to the health of English immigrants, was already declining, but a number of new towns had come into existence and the colonial population of the colony was more than four thousand and was growing rapidly.

The Chickahominy had been forced to move still farther inland, and had lost so much of their power and influence that their Confederation had disintegrated. But they were still the strongest Indian nation in the area.

Thomas Rolfe paid the first of many visits to the Chickahominy only a short time after his arrival, and was cordially greeted by his cousin, the son of Mataoko, who was now the Chief of the tribe. Piaoko, Thomas's uncle, was still alive, and had learned enough English to tell the young man about his mother's childhood and youth. The industrious Thomas, proud of his heritage, made it his business to learn the language of the Chickahominy, and in time spoke it fluently. His cousin, paid him a number of visits, and Piaoko so much enjoyed colonial ways that he came to the plantation house many times, often remaining for as long as a month or two.

In 1637 Thomas Rolfe was married to an English girl, the daughter of a minor member of the aristocracy who had migrated to Virginia with his family some years earlier. In

1640 Thomas and his wife, by then the parents of their first son, paid a visit to England of several months' duration.

Relations between King Charles and Parliament were deteriorating badly—the Civil War would break out in another two years—and although Thomas enjoyed visits with John and Barbara, life in England was not to his liking. Late in the year he returned to Virginia with his family and did not come back to England again.

Before his departure for home Thomas Rolfe made strenuous efforts to learn the nature of the illness that had killed his mother, but he was unsuccessful. Since that time a number of theories have been advanced. Until the present century it was popularly believed that she had died of consumption, but as she showed no symptoms of the disease that is unlikely. The real nature of the ailment that caused her swift and unexpected death remains as mysterious as many of the incidents in her life.

Thomas Rolfe became the wealthiest and one of the most influential tobacco planters in Virginia, and his sons followed in his footsteps. Down to the present day, the direct descendants of Pocahontas have played active roles in the affairs of Virginia and of the United States, proudly conscious of their precious and unique heritage.

BIBLIOGRAPHY

Arber, Edward, *Captain John Smith, a Critical Survey*, Birmingham, 1886.

Boyd, E., *The Story of Pocahontas and Captain John Smith*, London, 1905.

Bradley, A. G., *Captain John Smith*, London, 1905.

Breton, Nicholas, *The Courtier and the Countryman*, London, 1618.

Brown, Alexander, *The Genesis of the United States*, Boston, 1890.

Brown, John Carter, *New England's Trials*, London, 1867.

Chatterton, E. Kemble, *John Smith*, London, 1927.

Coates, Mary, *Social Life in Stuart England*, London, 1924.

Davies, G., *The Early Stuarts, 1603-1660*, London, 1937.

Deane, Charles, *Notes on Wingfield's Discourse on America*, Boston, 1859.

Doyle, Christina, *The English Housewife in the Seventeenth Century*, London, 1953.

Doyle, J. A., *English in America*, London, 1882.

Drummond, J. C., and Wilbram, Anne, *The Englishman's Food*, London, 1940.

Dyer, Frederick R., *The Pocahontas Myth*, Boston, 1901.

Fiske, John, *Old Virginia and Her Neighbors*, New York, 1897.

Forerunners and Competitors of the Pilgrims and Puritans, ed. by Charles Herbert Livermore, New York, 1912.

Fuller, Thomas, *Worthies of England*, ed. by John Freeman, London, 1952.

Gerson, Noel B., *Daughter of Eve*, New York, 1954.

, *Pocahontas*, New York, 1957.

Green, John Richard, A Short History of the English People, London, 1915.

Hart, Albert Bushnell, "American Historical Liars," *Harper's Magazine*, 1915.

Haydon, A. L., *Captain John Smith*, London, 1907.

Heydin, Peter, *Examen Historical, or a Discovery and Examination of the Mistakes, Falsities, and Defects in Some Modern Histories*, London, 1658-59.

Hilliard, George S., *The Life and Adventures of Captain John Smith*, Boston, 1834.

Hyle, Rita S., *Pocahontas, the Legend and the Reality*, Richmond, 1919.

Johnson, Rossiter, *Captain John Smith*, London, 1915.

Lewis, Paul, *The Great Rogue*, New York, 1966.

Neill, Edward Duffield, *English Colonization of America*, London, 1871.

, *Virginia Company in London*, London, 1869.

Neylor, George Thomas, *Pocahontas, the True and Untrue Stories and How they Grew*, Cambridge, 1889.

Palfrey, J. G., *History of New England*, Boston, 1858.

Peacham, Henry, *The Compleat Gentleman*, London, 1622.

Pelham, G. R., *The Life of Sir Thomas Dale, Bart.*, London, 1872.

Pirenne, Henry, *A History of Europe*, New York, 1938.

Poindexter, John, *Captain John Smith and His Critics*, London, 1893.

Roberts, E. P., *The Adventures of Captain John Smith*, London, 1902.

Smith, Bradford, *Captain John Smith*, Philadelphia, 1953.

Smith, John, *A True Relation of such occurrences and accidents of noat as hath happened in Virginia Since the First Planting of that Collony*, London, 1608.

, *A Map of Virginia, with a Description of the Countrey*, Oxford, 1612.

, *A Description of New England*, London, 1616.

, *The Generall Historie of Virginia, New England and the Summer Isles*, London, 1624.

, *The True Travels, Adventures, and Observations of Captaine John Smith*, London, 1630.

Tyler, Coit, *History of American Literature*, London, 1879.

Warner, Charles Dudley, *A Study of the Life and Writings of John Smith*, New York, 1881.

, *Pocahontas, the Indian Princess in Virginia and England*, New York, 1885.

Wharton, Henry, *The Life of John Smith*, translated from the Latin with an essay by Laura Polanyi Striker, Chapel Hill, N. C., 1957.

Winsor's History of America, ed. by Justin Winsor, Vols. I & III, Cambridge, 1889.

Woods, K. P., *The True Story of Captain John Smith, with Facts Relating to the Story of Pocahontas*, London, 1901.